**DO NOT REMOVE
CARDS FROM POCKET**

Presenting
the Macintosh

Merl K. Miller
Mary A. Myers

dilithium Press
Beaverton, Oregon

10   9   8   7   6   5   4   3   2   1

Library of Congress Catalog #84-5035

Cover: Christopher A. Dakan

Printed in the United States of America

dilithium Press
8285 S.W. Nimbus
Suite 151
Beaverton, Oregon 97005

Trademark Acknowledgements

2228822

Apple
Apple Computer
Apple II
Candy Apple
Chat
Cipher
CommQuest
CompuServe
Davong Systems
IBM
IBM PC
Lisa
Living Videotext
Lotus
Macintosh
Macintosh Logo
MacBASIC
MacFacts
MacPaint

MacPascal
MacWrite
MBASIC
Message Minder
Microsoft
MS-DOS
Multiplan
1-2-3
PC-DOS
PFS:FILE
Send Receive
Software Publishing
  Corporation
The Source
SPCA
Tecmar
Think Tank
VisiCalc

Acknowledgements

No one writes a book without help, especially a book about a new computer. We owe a debt of gratitude to those people who made this book possible:

To Pat Finnegan of dilithium Press, for learning MacPaint, drawing all of those pictures and writing the first draft of Chapter 6.

To Jody Gilbert, Jim Pierson and Vicki Tobin, all of dilithium Press, for making it all come together.

To Nancy Morrice of dilithium Press for her suggestions on how to improve the manuscript.

And

To Guy Kawasaki of Apple Computer for his technical help, his encouragement and the loan of a preproduction Macintosh.

Merl K. Miller

My thanks to Bob, for all his support and understanding.

Mary A. Myers

Contents

Chapter 1

Hello Mac

When Apple Computer introduced the Macintosh computer, the company provided an important link in a communications chain that began with Og the caveman. You remember old Og, don't you? Og went from campfire to campfire telling stories. He originated the concept of information management. When he didn't like the information he got, he changed it. Many of Og's descendants do the same thing today. The Og Jr.'s can really mess up the information flow of an organization. Now you can fight Ogism with the Mac.

The big problem with computers is they are stupid. In the old days, when you talked to Og, he could adapt as he went along. Maybe the information you got wasn't all that accurate, but he could speak your language. He might not have been very smart, but he was smarter than any computer you are likely to meet. Or, was he? If Og wanted to warn you to get inside before it rained, he might have said, "Rain god angry. Go to cave." English hadn't been invented yet, so he might have used sign language. He drew a visual image of what he wanted you to do. If you had to get this same information from a modern computer, the message would be, "Press F2 for rain and spell your name correctly. What would you like to do next?" Of course, if you don't spell your name correctly, you'll be left out in the rain. There must be a lot of people out there that didn't spell their names correctly. If you are one of them, have we got a pleasant surprise for you.

You may be wondering what all this has to do with the Macintosh. This is a different kind of computer. It is image-oriented. There are no complicated commands to learn, and there is very little to remember. If you want to write a letter to Aunt Gertrude, there is a picture of a piece of paper, with a hand holding a pencil. Now, if you want to see how effective this is, see if what you pictured in your mind is the same as the picture in the upper left corner of Figure 1.1. It would take several pages to describe everything in that picture, yet the picture itself takes only half a page. You get the idea.

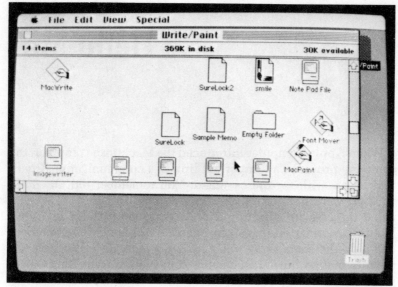

FIGURE 1.1

In this book, we'll describe the Macintosh and tell you why you might want to buy it. We'll tell you how it works. But this isn't a users' guide. We think buying the right computer is as important as learning to use it. We hope that, after you have finished this book, you will say to yourself: "This is a new technology. It isn't like other computers. Therefore, . . ." You'll have to fill in the therefore yourself. You may decide the Macintosh isn't what you want. This is fine with us, we have no connection with Apple. A word of warning, though, we love the Macintosh. It is really difficult to be cold and objective about the Mac, so at times our enthusiasm will leak through.

THE MACINTOSH HARDWARE

The Macintosh hardware shown in the Figure 1.2 consists of three pieces — the computer and monitor itself, the keyboard, and the mouse. We will describe these things in detail as we go along, and we will show you our own pictures. Now is probably a good

FIGURE 1.2

time to get a couple of terms straight. Hardware is the electronics, the plastic, and the metal that make up a computer. Software is the program or programs that make the computer do things. If you want an analogy, how about this one: hardware is a football team; software is the plays they run.

Of Mice and Windows

The Macintosh creates an *electronic desktop* where you do your work. You look in a *window* and manipulate things in the window with a mouse. The window concept is so important that we devoted Chapter 3 to windows and window manipulation. You will need a few concepts before you get to Chapter 3. First, you need to understand cut and paste. They mean exactly what you think. Electronically, you cut a piece of text or a picture out of something you are working on and paste it somewhere else. When you cut things, you place them on a *clipboard*. To paste something, you remove a copy from the clipboard. You also need to know about menus and the Finder. The Finder is a special program that helps you find things on your Macintosh. A menu is a list of options. The Finder menu is a list of options that help you find things on your Macintosh. So, you need to remember cut, paste, clipboard, Finder, and menu. Other than that, all you really need to know now is that you can use a window to look at what is on your desktop.

When we first heard about the mouse, we thought it was a gimmick. It's not. It's an easy, fast way to use the computer. You use a combination of special keys on most computers to do the things you do with the mouse on the Macintosh. Obviously, it's a lot easier for you to learn to use only one thing, the mouse, than to learn to use 20 special keys. Using a mouse feels weird at first. It doesn't go where you think it will go or where you want it to. It feels like peeling an apple with the wrong hand feels — very uncomfortable. At first, people find themselves clutching the mouse so tightly that their arms get tired from the effort. That is the inclination at first — to make the mouse go where you want it to go by sheer muscle power. However, after a bit of practice, using a mouse becomes as second-nature as using a pencil. The biggest problem you will have with using the mouse is trying to find a little open space on your desk. We have a friend who says an all-terrain rat would be more appropriate.

Concepts

Icons. On a real desktop, you work with one file for a while, then you go on to another, then maybe create a new file for different project. When you're finished working on one file, you need a convenient place to put it (like a file cabinet), where you can easily go back and get it when you need it. The Macintosh lets you do this, but the things you work with are represented with graphic images on Mac's electronic desktop. These images are called icons.

Mouse. Mac's mouse is the remote control. It's your key to working on the Mac desktop. Sliding the mouse on your real desktop moves the pointer on Mac's screen. You can slide the mouse in any direction, and the pointer moves the same distance in the same direction. The pointer is the arrow in Figure 1.3. Incidentally, we think using the terms pointer or arrow can be confusing, so we call it the mouse's tail.

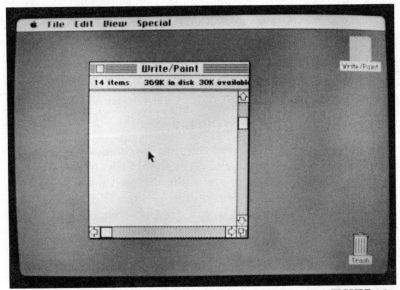

FIGURE 1.3

Click. When you slide the mouse, it moves the mouse's tail. Pressing the button on top of the mouse makes things happen. When you move the mouse's tail over an icon, then press and release the mouse button, the icon changes color. (The color is either black or white. The Macintosh displays only these two colors.) This press-and-release action is called clicking. When you click, you select an icon and it changes from white to black. To get anything more than that to happen, you have to specify an action (give a command). However, if you move the mouse's tail over an icon then press *and hold down* the mouse button, you can *drag* the icon to a new location by moving the mouse. As the mouse's tail moves, it drags an outline of the icon and its label along. The outline shows you where the icon will appear when you release the mouse button.

Choose From a Menu. With most other computers, you give a command by typing words or symbols with the keyboard. Remembering those commands is usually hard, if not impossible. With Mac you're never forced to memorize command words or type commands with the keyboard. Mac commands are listed in menus, and all you have to do is designate them with the mouse. You pull menus down onto the screen with the mouse when you need them. They don't intrude when you don't need them, but they're right there when you do.

There are some common complaints about menus: they're too slow, once you've learned the ropes; they monopolize the screen; and you usually end up typing in a code number or letter. But Macintosh menus are unobtrusive and fast, and no typing is necessary.

WHAT'S IN THE REST OF THIS BOOK?

We hope we haven't confused you with the computer and Macintosh jargon we have introduced. This should become clear as we go along. The Macintosh is a visually oriented machine, so we will illustrate everything we can with pictures. If it's true that a picture is worth a thousand words, then we have cut way down on your reading time.

The next chapter describes the Macintosh desk accessories. These are some of our favorite features. You will find out about things like the calculator, the clock and the puzzle.

Chapter 3 tells you more about the Macintosh windows. It may be the most important chapter in the book. If you can understand the concept of windows, you will be able to evaluate the Macintosh and compare it with other computers.

MacWrite and MacPaint were the first programs introduced for the Macintosh. It is a word processing program. In case you are unfamiliar with word processing, some word processing fundamentals are introduced in Chapter 4. This chapter also will give you some guidelines for evaluating word processing programs and word processors. MacWrite is described in Chapter 5.

If you would like to learn how to draw great business graphics, you'll like MacPaint. You can use it to draw everything from organization charts, to bar graphs, to cows and flowers. You are right, of course, cows and flowers aren't business graphics, but do you have to be serious all of the time? Chapter 6 will introduce you to MacArtistry.

While we don't claim to be seers, we do have a crystal ball. We have read a large pile of press releases, and we have talked to people at 80 companies about what they are developing for the Mac. We have some predictions in Chapter 7.

The computer business seems overladen with jargon, so we have included a glossary at the end.

WHAT MAC CANNOT DO

There is no such thing as a perfect computer, and there probably never will be. The Macintosh is no exception. It does have limitations. There are two things about the Mac we don't like — color and memory.

The Macintosh displays everything in black and white. This is not a serious limitation when you look at the intended audience. Few business applications require color. However, many business applications can be enhanced by color. You can compensate for lack of color with shading, but it's just not the same thing. Apple plans to make color available for the Macintosh, but it is a difficult technical problem. You'll begin to understand how serious this problem is when you read Chapter 6 on MacPaint. All we need to say here is that the Macintosh display is quite complex. Adding color to the display would add another layer of complexity.

The second problem is a greater limitation, but it's easier to solve. The Macintosh has only 128K of RAM. (How's that for a technical sentence?) RAM, or random access memory, is the computer's internal memory. You store things in RAM as you work with the computer. K is a measure of the amount of memory available. It stands for 1024 bytes of memory. A byte of memory represents 1 character, space or symbol in memory. Whew! So, if you have 128K of RAM, you can store about 128,000 characters a time. A page in this book is about 2500 characters, and an average business letter is about 1000 characters. You could store 52 pages of this book or 128 business letters in the Macintosh computer at one time, if you could store the program somewhere else. Most Macintosh programs use about 100K of memory. With what's left, you might be able to store a long business letter, but you can't store a magazine article or a chapter of a book.

You may think we are being a little too picky about this memory problem, and you are probably right. Most of what we do with our computers involves book chapters, long articles and mammoth financial projections. There is a very good chance that none of this will affect you. Besides that, Apple should have this problem solved by the summer of 1984. It is our understanding that the company expects to offer a Macintosh with 512K of memory. Apple also will offer an upgrade, so if you buy a 128K Macintosh, you can take it to your dealer and have it upgraded into a 512K Macintosh. Apple has been pretty good about this sort of thing in the past, so it should involve only nominal cost.

We don't think either color or memory problems are serious limitations of an otherwise great computer, but you will have to evaluate that yourself. If you are ready to give managerial computing a try, we suggest you take a close look at the Macintosh.

Okay, let's take a look at the desk accessories.

Chapter 2

The Macintosh
Desk Accessories

The Apple people may not know what they have here. We doubt you will see very much advertising or review space devoted to the desk accessories. However, you will probably appreciate this feature more than any other. The desk accessories are a group of things everybody has always wanted on a computer. Each one is unique. The clock, the calculator and the notepad replace things you have on your desk now. The scrapbook is something you probably should have. Key caps and the control panel both help you use your computer more effectively. Then there's the puzzle. It's primary purpose is to drive you insane, or give you something to do while you are on hold, or give you an alternative to doodling, or maybe all of the above. Notepad and scrapbook are both files, so they can be moved from one disk to another. The desk accessories are represented on the left of the screen beneath the apple, as in Figure 2.1. We'll start by describing notepad, because it has the most uses.

NOTEPAD

Remember how your high school English teacher used to tell you to make an outline as the first step in writing anything? It is a good idea, but few people do it. You probably use some kind of notes, instead. You may keep the notes in your head, or you may scratch them out on a piece of paper. Even if you use a computer now, you probably do your note scratching or your outlining on a piece of paper. Then, when you are ready to write something, you have to try to find the piece of paper. If you are one of those

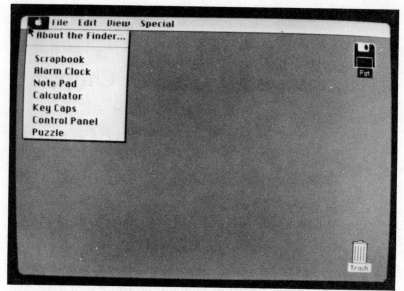

FIGURE 2.1

super-neat people, you know right where it is. However, if you were nodding your head in agreement with me a second ago, you may need a better system. Even if you never write anything, you may need a better system of keeping track of your notes, or your appointments, or who you are supposed to call tomorrow. You can do all of those things with notepad. Anything you write on the notepad can be transferred to other files or programs.

Chapters 5 and 6 are devoted to writing, so we won't dwell on that here. Figures 2.2 and 2.3 show how we used the notepad function to help develop this chapter. The first figure is page 1 of the notepad. We wrote some notes about what we wanted to cover in this chapter and why. The second figure is a rough outline of the chapter. We actually went into more detail on other pages, but you get the idea.

The notepad can't replace a leather bound appointment book and an excellent secretary, but it can help you get a little more organized. There are eight pages in the notepad. Figure 2.4 is an example of a things-to-do list. You can keep this for eight consecutive days.

SCRAPBOOK

The scrapbook is a place to store information that you may want to use over and over again with different projects. For instance,

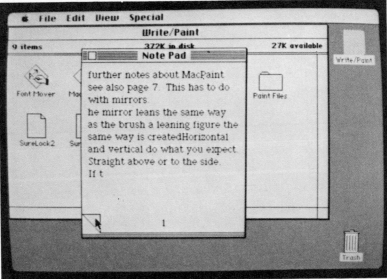

FIGURE 2.2

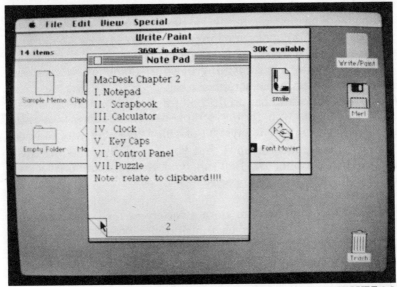

FIGURE 2.3

you could have a group of common business phrases you want to put in every letter you write. They can be created with either the notepad or with MacWrite. Then, when you want to use one of those phrases, you call up the appropriate scrapbook page and

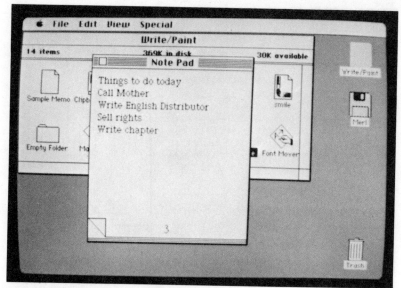

FIGURE 2.4

paste the phrase into your letter. Most of what you write in your notepad will change frequently. However, you can maintain something in your scrapbook for a long time. There is even a technique for creating several different scrapbooks.

Each time you put something in your scrapbook, it creates a new page. Pages in the scrapbook can be erased using the clear command. The scroll bar on the bottom of the icon indicates your approximate location in the scrapbook. Also, there is a page counter (for example, it says: 03 of 10). There's no way to erase the entire scrapbook at once. But you can throw it in the trash and get another one. The first time you see the scrapbook, it will display the following five pages:

1. Use the Scrapbook to store a variety of text selections and pictures which may be transferred between applications. From the edit menu, cut or copy an item from the Scrapbook, then paste into an application document.
2. A picture of a fish as shown in Figure 2.5.
3. The knots shown in Figure 2.6.
4. The friendly robot in Figure 2.7.
5. The fleur de lance in Figure 2.8.

Any of these items can be pasted into an application program. For instance, you can paste the robot into MacPaint. This gives

FIGURE 2.5

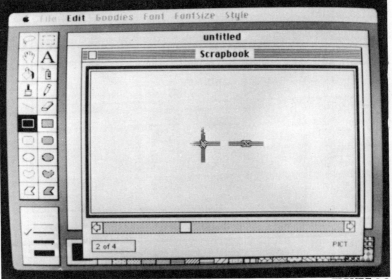

FIGURE 2.6

you an opportunity to see how it was drawn. Once you understand
how someone else draws things with MacPaint, it is much easier
to figure out how to do it yourself. We tried to draw our own
robot. Our *Country Robot* is shown in Figure 2.9. We are particu-
larly proud of the shoes.

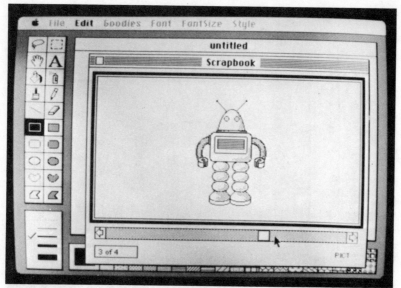

FIGURE 2.7

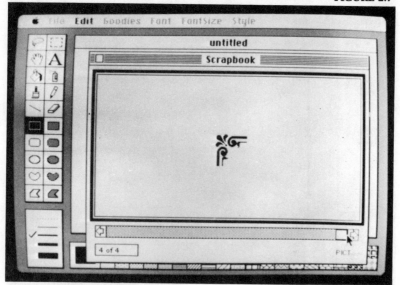

FIGURE 2.8

You can put things in the scrapbook any place you want them by going to the page you want and pasting it there. Other pages are advanced a notch to accommodate your newly added page. You can't write things in your scrapbook. They have to be created somewhere else and pasted in, just like with a real scrapbook. If

FIGURE 2.9

you paste something in your scrapbook that is longer than one page, Macintosh creates a second page for the extra material.

CALCULATOR

This is a standard four-function calculator. The only operational diference between the Macintosh calculator and a standard four-function calculator is the Mac's version uses * instead of × for multiplication. There are several ways you can use it. Using the screen display of the calculator keyboard, you can point with the mouse's tail to the key you want and push the mouse button. This is great for impressing your friends and wowing your office mates, but it is inefficient. You can also use the keyboard keys or the numeric keypad. The C and E keys on Mac's keyboard work the same as keys lettered that way on some calculators. C clears the display. E is scientific notation for 1000. If you type 2E + 3 and press the equals sign, the computer displays 2000. This real handy if you are going to use large numbers. For instance, the cost of one B-1 bomber is $1,000,000,000. This can be displayed as 1E + 9. The cost of two B-1 bombers, therefore, is 2E + 9. The cost of three B-1 bombers, of course, is ludicrous.

You can paste numbers from other documents into the calculator and paste them back when you're through calculating. If you want to solve a long, complicated problem, you can put the elements on the notepad then solve the problem with the calculator. The nice thing about this is that you can edit the problem as you go. This means you can backspace, erase and insert. Haven't you always wanted to do that on a calculator? You can check the problem before and after the calculation if you leave the clipboard out. For instance, you can type this on the notepad: 3.14*22 + (93.18/63). Then you can copy it to the clipboard and paste it into the calculator. The calculator displays the answer, not the calculation. You can then copy the answer back to the notepad. This isn't the ultimate solution to how you mix numbers and words in the same document, but it will work.

ALARM CLOCK

The nice thing about the Macintosh desk accessories is they work like you expect them to. This is especially true of the alarm clock. Figure 2.10 shows the display. Did you notice the lever in the upper right hand corner? When you push the lever with the mouse's tail, you get the display shown in Figure 2.11. Now you can adjust the time or the date or you can set the alarm clock. When you select the alarm clock, you get the display shown in Figure 2.12. Notice the button on the left. You use it to set the alarm. It works like the button on the back of your regular alarm clock. When it is down, the alarm is off. When it is up, the alarm

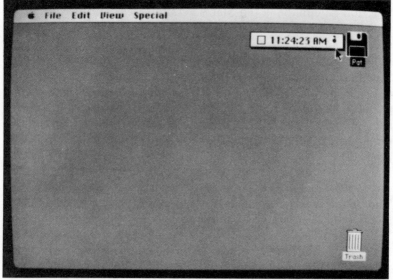

FIGURE 2.10

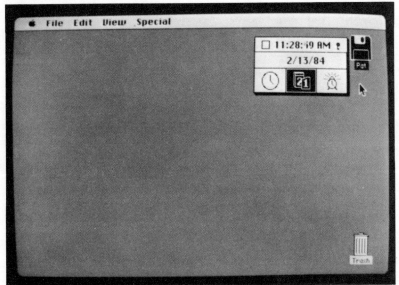

FIGURE 2.11

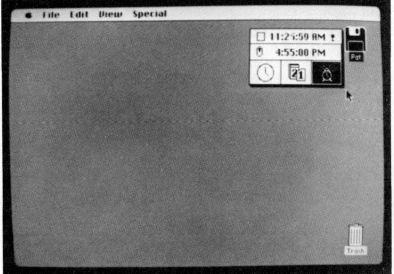

FIGURE 2.12

is on. When you select an option, the hour for instance, two arrows
appear on the right side of the display. You can now adjust the
setting with your mouse's tail. This is shown in Figure 2.13. The
alarm rings at the appointed time. The internal buzzer beeps once,

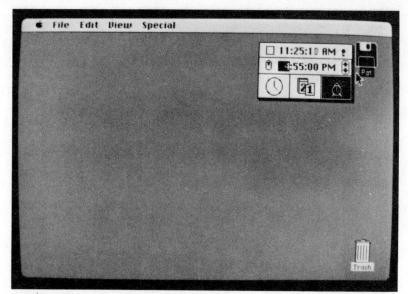

FIGURE 2.13

and the desk accessory apple blinks. The apple continues to blink until you turn the alarm off.

The Macintosh automatically stamps every document you create with the date and time. This is a real boon to the disorganized. We are constantly creating files with the same contents but different names. With other computers, it can be a long, tedious process sorting through things until you find the latest version. With the Mac, you just check to see which file has the latest date and time. If you want, you can even make it an actual part of the file. All you have to do is open the clock and select the cut function from the edit menu. The date and time are cut to the clipboard. They can be pasted into your document in the same way anything else is.

KEY CAPS

The Macintosh draws everything, including letters, on the screen. We'll explain this in a little more detail in Chapter 6. What is important here is that all non-control keys except the space bar and backspace have multiple purposes. The keyboard is shown in Figure 2.14. The control keys are tab, caps lock, shift, option, command, enter, and return. The tab key is on the upper left. Starting with the tab key, you can find the other control keys by looking down the keyboard, then right and finally up. The command key is between the option key and the space bar.

FIGURE 2.14

When you choose key caps from the menu, you get the display shown in Figure 2.15. Now you can press a control key and display another set of characters. The shift key and caps lock are the same as on a typewriter. The shifted keys are shown in Figure 2.16. Enter and return keys have no effect on what is displayed. The command key doesn't either. The option key gives you the set of keys displayed in Figure 2.17. If you press both shift and option at the same time, you get the keys shown in Figure 2.18.

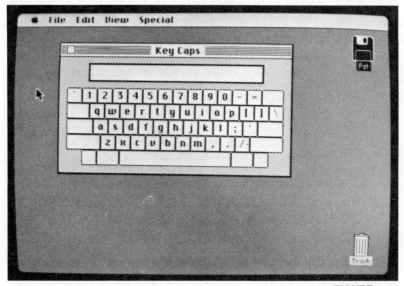

FIGURE 2.15

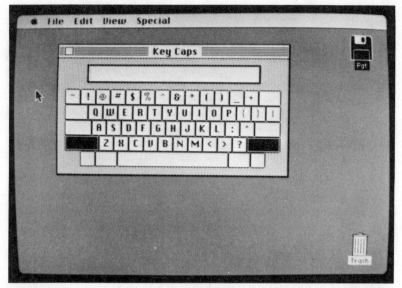

FIGURE 2.16

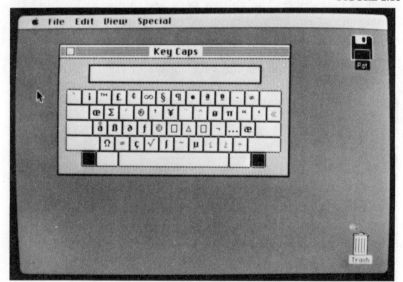

FIGURE 2.17

Now, how can you use this? Let's say you are writing a letter to your British distributor. You know the Macintosh has a £ key, but you don't remember where it is. If you call up key caps and press the option key you will see that it is the 3 key. All you have to do to insert it in your text is press the option key and the 3

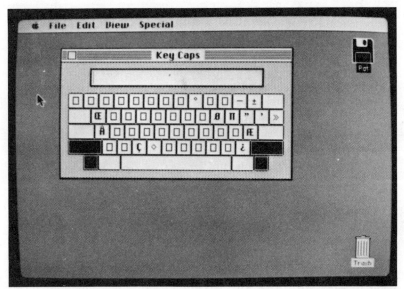

FIGURE 2.18

key. Of course, if you can remember all the different keys, you won't use the key caps display feature.

CONTROL PANEL

You can change anything from how fast you want the cursor to blink to how loudly the bell rings. Here are the things you can control:

1. Bell. Settings are from 0 to 7. The 0 setting is no sound. The 7 setting is a little louder than most telephones.
2. Date and time. You can also set these when you look at the clock.
3. Command blinking rate. When you use the mouse to pull down a command, the command is highlighted. This controls how often a command blinks when you select it. This is really handy when you are learning the computer. If you set it at the high rate of three initially, you have time to look at your selection before it is enacted.
4. Keys. You can determine how fast you want keys to respond. If you are a fast typist, you might want the keyboard to accommodate light, rapid keystrokes and to rebound quickly. If you are a slow typist, you might want the keys to rebound only after a short pause and to avoid repeating letters in the meantime.

5. Cursor blink. There are three settings. The slow setting will probably put you to sleep. It blinks once every second and a half. This might seem fast, but once you get used to your computer, it seems like the cursor is never going to blink on this setting. The fast setting makes the cursor blink about two times a second. This seems a little frantic to us. However, if you are really high-charged, you might like it. The medium setting blinks steadily once per second. That's about our speed.

6. Mouse controls. There are two mouse controls. A double-click option controls the length of time between double clicks. There is also a speed control. The 1 setting is twice as fast as the 0 setting. We will explain how this works in Chapter 6.

PUZZLE

This is like the little puzzles with sliding plastic pieces that you used to play with as a kid. Except this one is somewhat more frustrating. There is no way to solve the puzzle fraudulently by prying up the pieces. Apple claims the puzzle lets you relax during your business day. We don't believe this claim. Actually, it is probably a fiendishly clever plot to outsmart IBM. Apple probably plans to sell Macintoshes to all IBM upper-level managers. Then, while they're trying to solve the Apple puzzle, Apple will design new computers. This is a logical conclusion when you think about it. IBM has been trying to solve the Apple puzzle for several years now.

We have shown an unsolved puzzle in Figure 2.19 and a solved one in Figure 2.20. What we can't show you is the way it flashes when you get it right or the essence of sheer joy we experienced when we solved it.

SUMMARY

The Macintosh desk accessories add an extra dimension to an already remarkable computer. There has never been a computer in this price range that would do all of these things. Apple has given a lot of thought to how people really work. As a result, it has included this group of commonly used desk items. The accessories will help you organize your work and give you more time to be both creative and productive.

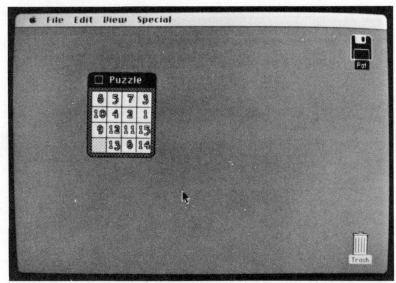

FIGURE 2.19

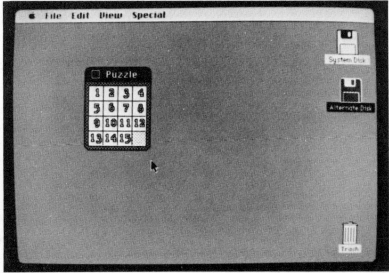

FIGURE 2.20

Chapter 3

A Window on the World

What do you see when you look out your window? It probably depends on what window. If you look out the window at your office, you might see trees, flowers, people or an industrial complex. At home, you might see something entirely different. What would people see if they looked in your window? In particular, what would you see if you looked at your desk through a window? That is what you are going to do with the Macintosh. This is your big chance to be a peeping Tom (or Karen, or Fred, or Matilda).

Here is the fun part — you get a whole bunch of windows. You can look in any one of them at any time. The Macintosh draws a window on the screen for any application you want to use. Several windows can be on the screen at once. This means you can look at the contents of several files at once. The information in a window can be a document, a request for more information, or a dialog box. The sizes of the windows can be changed, and windows can be split to show different parts of a document simultaneously. Information from one window, or application, can be moved to another. This makes it easy to create reports that use combinations of numbers, text and graphics.

Let's take a little closer look at your desk. In the upper left is a stack of file folders. Okay, that makes sense. On the right, you have an *In* basket and an *Out* basket. In the middle you have a pile of papers you are working on and a two-week-old cheese sandwich. Not too neat, but you like it. You can put most of that stuff in your Macintosh, and you can use the same system you use now. You can have things in your file folders and the file folders in a stack. You can have quickly scribbled notes. You can have a cheese sandwich. You'll have to draw it with MacPaint, so it won't be edible, but the one you have now isn't edible either. You can arrange your electronic desktop any way you want and use the windows to work on the things you've accumulated. We'll peek through some Macintosh windows in this chapter.

ADJUSTING THE WINDOW

The Macintosh desktop starts off nice and clean, but you can mess it up if you want. Figure 3.1 shows the first desktop you'll see when you load your system disk. Across the top of the screen, you see the standard Finder menus. The little apple represents the desk accessories. File gives you access to documents, files and programs. Edit helps you manipulate documents and files. View arranges your window for you, and Special empties the trash, cleans up your desk and erases your files. We'll examine these menus in detail once you have had a chance to look in a window.

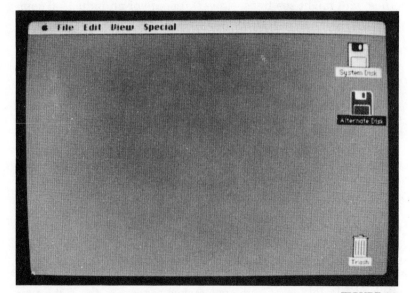

FIGURE 3.1

On the right of the screen, you see a picture of a disk. A little box under it is labeled *System Disk*. This tells you the system disk is available. On the bottom right of the screen, you'll discover that trash is also available. This is where the cheese sandwich goes. Apple calls these pictures icons. Our dictionary defines an icon as an object of uncritical devotion. (Apple may have gone too far with this one.) Some dictionaries also define it as an emblem or symbol. The Macintosh uses icons to picture things available to you. If you want to actually work with one of those things, you have to open a window. This makes sense if you think about it. When you want to get something that's on the other side of a window, you have to open it. The fastest way to open a window, is to stick the mouse's tail in it and hit the mouse button twice. As you might expect, the window turns black the first time you hit the mouse and it opens the second time. You can also hit the mouse button once and then choose to open from the file menu. This is a little more cumbersome, but the SPCA likes it better.

Let's open the system disk window and see what happens. As you can see in Figure 3.2, a window labelled System Disk has opened in the upper left of the screen. It looks more like a desk pad than a window, but you can't have everything. An information line tells you eight items are in the window. These require 217K of memory on the disk. As each disk holds 400K, you have 183K available for your use.

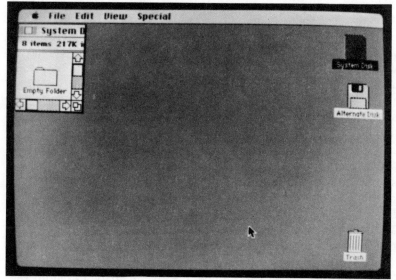

You can make the window any size you want. Notice the two little squares on the bottom right of the window. If you put the mouse's tail in a box and pull the mouse towards you, the window gets larger. If you push it away, the window gets smaller. If you pull to the right it expands to the right. If you pull straight down, it expands down. You get the idea. As you can see in Figure 3.3,

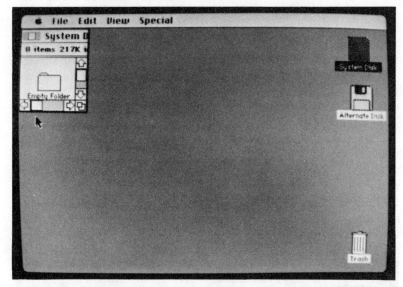

FIGURE 3.3

we have made our window quite small. If you look closely at the window, you will see something new. There is a little box right above the mouse's tail. This is your window on Mac's world. It shows you what part of the whole you can see. It is called a scroll box. The box is on the far left of the window, so you are seeing the far left side only. In Figure 3.4, you can see the center.

With a little mouse magic, we can rearrange the icons so they are in a column, as in Figure 3.5. Now, when we make the window small, there is an addition. There is a little window on the right of the screen. This window can be moved up and down. Using these little windows, you can have a tiny window on your screen and still look at everything on your disk. And yes, you are right, the arrows do move the little windows.

The windows not only can be adjusted but also can be moved. If you put the mouse's tail anywhere in the striped area on the top of the screen and hold the button, the window moves when you move the mouse. We are in the process of moving a window in Figure 3.6. Windows can be moved to any place on the screen, even when only part of the window will show after the move. We have moved most of our window off the screen in Figure 3.7.

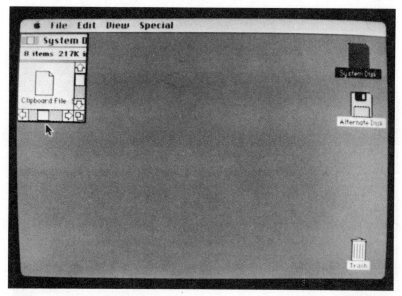

FIGURE 3.4

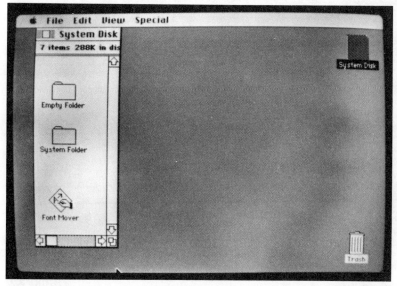

FIGURE 3.5

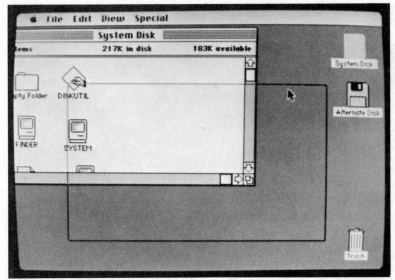

FIGURE 3.6

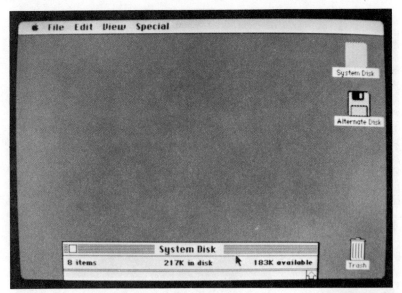

FIGURE 3.7

THE DESKTOP

One of the really nice things about the Macintosh is you can have either a clean desk or a messy desk. As you know, there is nothing in between. Since we prefer a messy desk, we changed disks. The rest of our illustrations are from our Write disk. You will learn about MacWrite and MacPaint in the next three chapters, so we won't talk about them here. We selected the Write disk because it is messy and it has a lot of things on it. In all fairness though, we should tell you it wasn't messy when we got it from Apple.

On a real desk, you can move things around and put them where you want. You can do this with the Macintosh too. Just stick the mouse's tail in what you want, hit the mouse button and make the move. Icons inside the window work the same as icons outside. Push the mouse button and they turn black. Push the mouse button again and a window opens. You can have a whole bunch of windows open at the same time. In Figure 3.8, we have five windows open. The top window is called the active window. You can move things from the active window to other windows, or you can open files in the active window. We'll close all windows except Write/Paint.

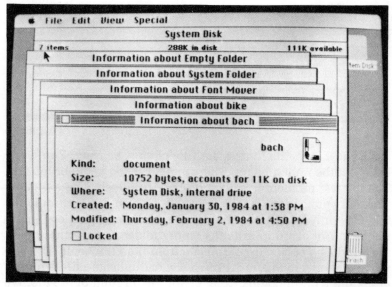

FIGURE 3.8

There are six files in the window that we never actually open
— Finder, System, Note Pad, Scrapbook, Clipboard, and Imagewriter. These files are used indirectly. For instance, the contents
of the notepad are stored in the Note Pad file. We may want to
transfer these files to another disk but, in the meantime, they are
just in the way. One solution is to stack them in the corner as we
have done in Figure 3.9. Of course, it is kind of hard to see what
is in the pile, and it still takes up some desk space. What do you
do with files that you don't use all the time? If you want to keep
them handy,you put them in a file drawer in your desk. This is
exactly what we do with the Macintosh files. We put our six system
files in a folder.

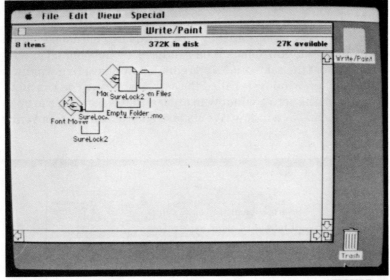

FIGURE 3.9

As you know, file folders are like clothes hangers. You never
have just the right amount. There are either too many or too few.
The *too few* problem is solved on the Macintosh. The *too many*
problem you'll have to solve yourself. One empty electronic file
folder is provided by the Mac. It is actually a bottomless empty
file box. You can duplicate the empty folder or any other file in
the window by selecting Duplicate from the File menu. The File
menu is shown in Figure 3.10. When you duplicate a file, a replica
of the file with the prefix *Copy of* appears in front of the file. We
have shown this in Figure 3.11. In Figure 3.12, we changed the

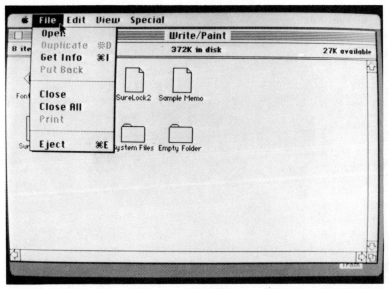

FIGURE 3.10

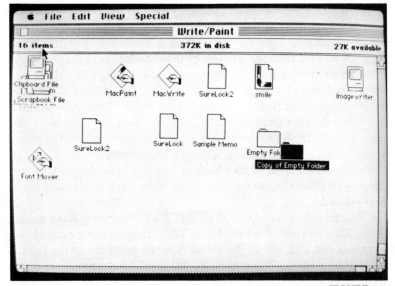

FIGURE 3.11

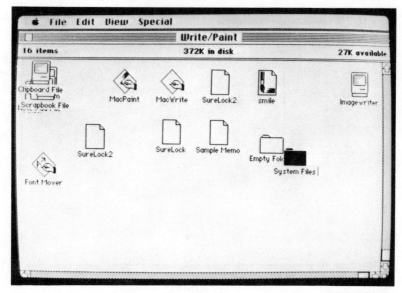

FIGURE 3.12

name of this new folder to *System Files*. This is easy. All you have to do is make the icon black, and type the name you want.

Now we can put our files in the System Files folder. There are two ways to do this. You can stick files into a folder in the Macintosh anytime you want to. If you drag a file to a folder and let go of the mouse button, the file is put into the folder. You can move all the system files into the folder at once or put them there one at a time. Normally, we would move them as a group, but it is easier to show you how this works if we move them individually. Before we do this though, we'll have to clean up our desk. The Special menu is shown in Figure 3.13. The first item on the menu is Clean Up. This command tells the Macintosh to put the icons in neat rows. It is sort of like having a nice efficient secretary that straightens things up once in a while. Our desk is cleaned up in Figure 3.14.

In Figure 3.15, we show the Note Pad file being filed in the folder. This is kind of a neat trick. We can keep our notepad in a file folder and still use it. Better yet, we can keep several notepads in the folder at one time. All we have to do is give each one a different name. We have already put the System file, the Finder file and the Imagewriter file in the folder.

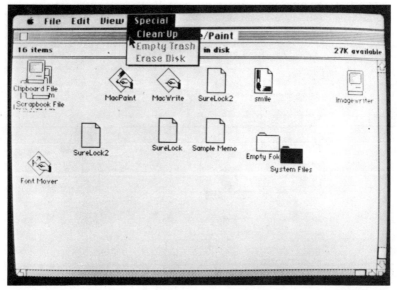

FIGURE 3.13

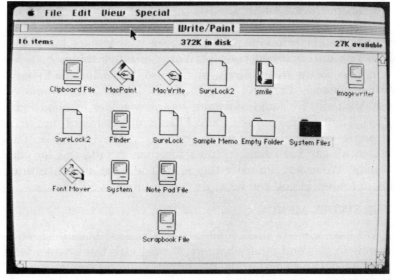

FIGURE 3.14

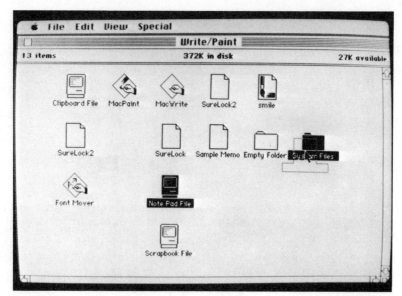

FIGURE 3.15

We'll use a different method to put the Scrapbook file and the Clipboard file in the folder. In Figure 3.16, we have opened the System files window and adjusted the size of both windows. Now, we can move the Clipboard file and the Scrapbook file to the System file window. This is shown in Figure 3.17. You probably won't use this technique to file things in your folders, but it does illustrate an important concept. You can move things between windows easily. In addition, you can use this technique to move things between disks. As an example, in Figure 3.18, we moved our MacPaint files and MacPaint to a new folder labelled *Paint Files*. Then we moved the Paint Files icon outside of the Write window. We can open either one or both whenever we like. This means we can keep similar things together. We did this for your benefit. We're not normally this neat. The most attractive thing about folders is you can be as tidy or untidy as you like.

THE FINDER MENUS

We have already used some of the standard Macintosh commands in this and other chapters. We'll finish this chapter with a review of these commands. It is important to remember, though, that each application will have a menu of its own, and may or may not use all of these commands. For instance, MacWrite has

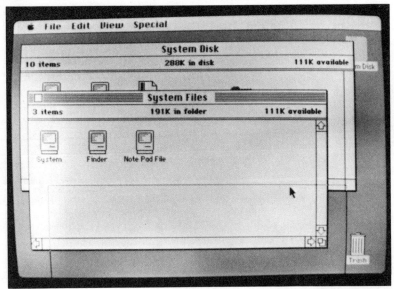

FIGURE 3.16

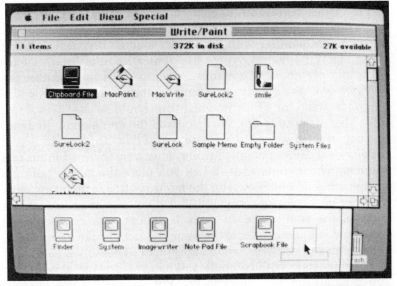

FIGURE 3.17

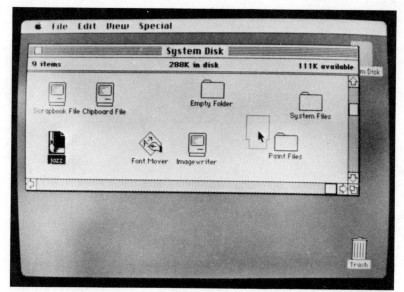

FIGURE 3.18

the desk accessories menu, a File menu, and an Edit menu. It also has a Search menu, a Format menu, a Font menu and a Style menu. The File and Edit menus have some of the same commands as the Finder menus, but they are not identical. This may sound confusing, but it's not. Menus are used in a consistent manner so, once you are familiar with the Finder menus, it is easy to begin using MacWrite menus. Apple has done a lot to make it easy for software developers to use this concept. All of the applications software we have seen uses menus in these consistent ways. If you understand the Finder menus, you should be able to evaluate most Macintosh software. We discussed the apple menu in detail in Chapter 2, so we will start here with File.

Before we discuss menus further, however, we need to make a comment about commands. When you place the mouse tail on a menu name and hold down on the mouse button, a menu appears. You can now select a command. But there also are shortcuts for some of the commands. In some instances, you can press the command key and a letter at the same time and evoke a command. (The command key is shown in Figure 3.19.) This solves a problem most people have with computers. When you first use a computer, you need all the help you can get. But, as you become familiar with the computer, you don't want to go through a long, tedious

FIGURE 3.19

menu process to do your work. What you really need is some way to shortcut the process once you have learned how to use the computer or program. Often times, the shortcut is so arcane that it is easier to do it the slow way. The Macintosh shortcuts are fairly straightforward. If you want information, you press the *I* key and the Command key at the same time. If you want to duplicate something, you press the *D* key and the Command key. It will still take some time to learn the shortcuts, but at least they make sense. We'll introduce each shortcut when we describe the command.

File

The File menu is shown in Figure 3.10. You can use *Open* to open an application program, a folder or a file. For instance, if you want to open MacWrite, you can stick the mouse's tail on the MacWrite icon and click the button once. Then, you can select Open from the File menu. You can shortcut this procedure by double clicking the mouse button.

We introduced *Duplicate* when we duplicated the empty folder. Keep in mind that anything in the window can be duplicated then moved to a folder, another window or another disk. The shortcut for Duplicate is *Command D.*

If you are already somewhat familiar with computers, you have probably noticed the *Get Info* command. We do a lot of word processing, so this was the first command we played with. Oftentimes when you do word processing, you need to create backup files. As you can see in Figure 3.20, we have two files with similar names: SureLock and SureLock2. SureLock2 is our backup. If we were well organized and prudent, SureLock2 would always be exactly the same as SureLock. We are seldom organized and prudent, so sometimes we don't know which file is the latest. We can use the information command to look at SureLock2. The window in Figure 3.21 tells us SureLock2 is a document created on Sunday, February 5, 1984 at 1:35 p.m. and that it was modified on Friday, February 8, 1984 at 10:09 a.m. It also tells us SureLock2 is on the Write/Paint disk we have in the internal drive and it takes up 4498 bytes of memory. Now, we can move the information window down to the bottom of the screen and get the same information about SureLock. If we position the windows carefully, we can look at the information for both files at the same time. In fact, we can put the information for up to seven files on the screen at one time. This is shown in Figure 3.22. You can use *Command I* as a shortcut for this command.

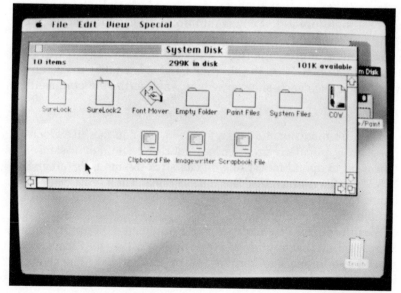

FIGURE 3.20

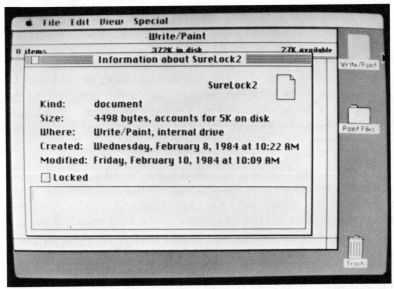

FIGURE 3.21

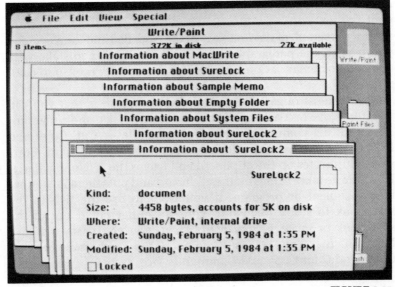

FIGURE 3.22

The Put Back command returns files to their original window when you change your mind. As an example, if you put something in the trash then decide you really want to keep it, you can put it back.

There are three ways to close a window when you are through with it. You will probably use the shortcut most of the time. All you have to do is stick the mouse's tail in the little box in the upper left of the window and click the mouse button. If you want to take a little more time, you can select *Close* from the File menu. If you have more than one window open, you can select *Close All* from the File menu and close all the windows.

When you are finished, you need a way to get your disk out of the computer. Once you have closed all the files you can select *Eject* from the File menu or press *Command E*. The computer ejects the disk. It is kind of surprising the first time it happens. We are used to computers that have a disk drive door. There is always a little hassle getting the disk in and out of the drive in most computers. It took us about three seconds to decide we like the Macintosh system a lot better.

Edit

The Edit menu, shown in Figure 3.23, is used to edit the names of icons, change text in an information window, and alter text or pictures in a desk accessory. The first command, *Undo*, undoes your last text editing. For instance, suppose you decided to erase the last paragraph of the first page of the Note Pad and then decided you needed the paragraph. You could rectify this mistake with the Undo command. *Command Z* is a shortcut for the Undo command.

One of the strongest features of the Macintosh is that you can use it to move text among files, documents, disks, and programs. Three editing commands make this possible — *Cut, Copy* and *Paste*. Cut removes material and stores it on the clipboard. Copy stores duplicates on the clipboard and leaves the original material intact. Paste takes things off the clipboard and puts them in another file, document or program. If you want to use the fish in the scrapbook to study MacPaint, you can either cut it out of the scrapbook or make a copy of it. Then, you can paste it into a MacPaint file. You can use *Command X* as a shortcut for Cut, *Command C* for Copy and *Command V* for Paste.

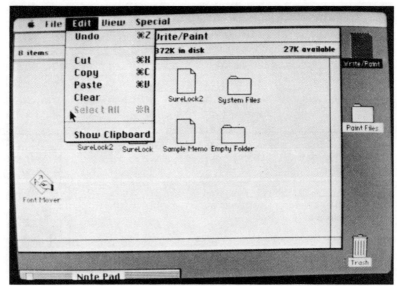

FIGURE 3.23

The *Clear* command is a big eraser. It will clean up what you are working on. If you want to erase a page of the scrapbook, for example, you can find the page and erase it with Clear. You don't want a shortcut for Clear, so there isn't one. A shortcut just gives you one more chance to erase something you didn't want erased.

Select All selects all icons in the active window. This makes it easy to move all icons to another window, to get information about them, etc. *Command A* is a shortcut for Select All.

You probably are tired of hearing about the clipboard, so we won't dwell on it here. You can use the *Show Clipboard* command to learn what you cut or copied to the clipboard. There is a clipboard showing in Figure 3.24.

View

When you open a window, icons are displayed for documents, files, folders and programs. This is the easiest way to work with a window, but there may be times you need more information about your files. In Figure 3.25, we have made the window about the same size as the screen and have displayed the View menu. The check mark by the command by Icon indicates everything is displayed by icon. Figure 3.26 shows the window contents dis-

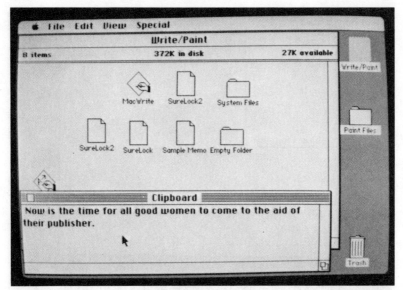

FIGURE 3.24

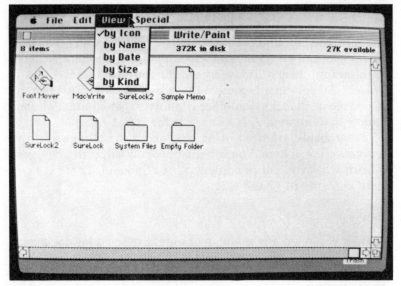

FIGURE 3.25

played *by Name*. This gives most of the information you get when
you use the Get Info command on the File menu. It tells you at a
glance what you have in this window. The *by Date* command
gives you the display in Figure 3.27. In particular, you might look

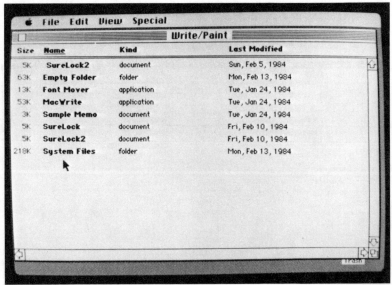

FIGURE 3.26

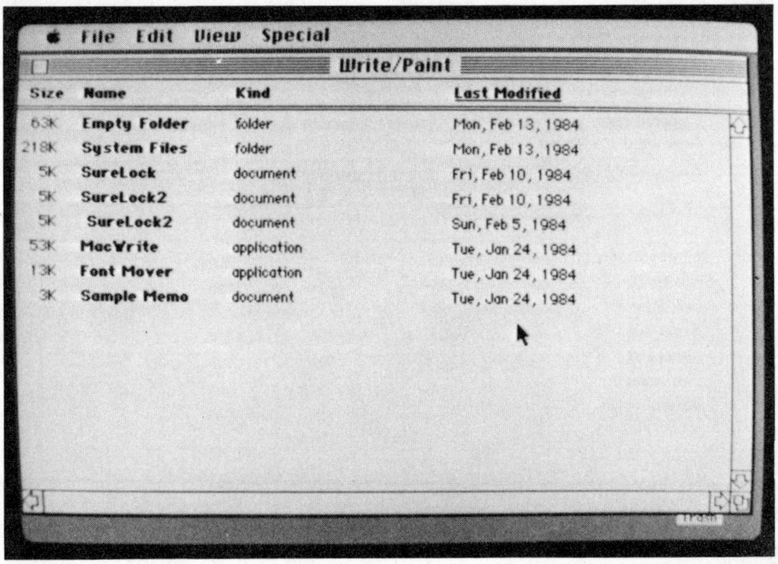

FIGURE 3.27

at the dates for SureLock and SureLock2. We can easily see which
document was worked on last. The *by Size* command is extremely
helpful when you are trying to decide which files you want to
transfer to another disk. We have displayed the files by size in

Figure 3.28. The *by Kind* command is also an excellent aid for determining what should and should not be on a particular disk. Figure 3.29 shows our Write/Paint disk files displayed by kind.

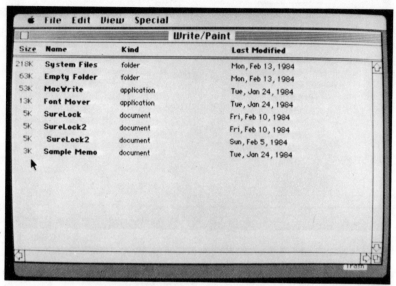

FIGURE 3.28

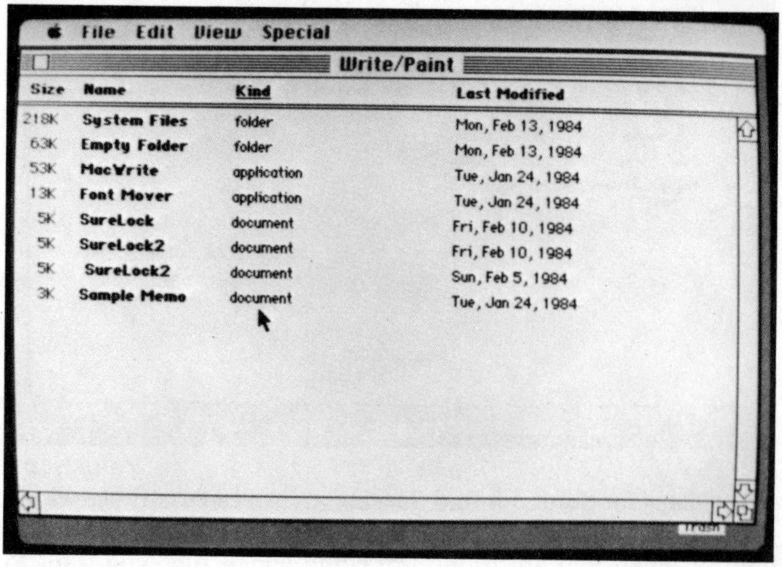

FIGURE 3.29

Special

We introduced the *Clean Up* command when we discussed folders. Clean up is the first command in the Special menu shown in Figure 3.13. This command rearranges the icons so that they are easier to read and use. Figure 3.30 shows a mess we made to illustrate this point, and Figure 3.31 shows the Clean Up command in action.

It would do you no good to throw things in the trash if there weren't a way to empty the trash. When you want to discard something, you open the Trash window and move the throw-away files to the trash. The *Empty Trash* command is the janitor. When you select it, whatever you have in the trash is thrown away permanently. Speaking of throwing things away permanently, there is another command on the Special menu: *Erase Disk*. We are so paranoid about losing things that we haven't tried this command yet. We don't intend to for a while. We assume it does just what it says. We'll try it out the next time we clean our desks (the wooden ones).

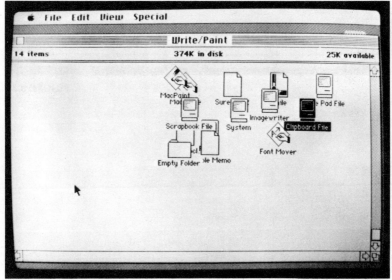

FIGURE 3.30

This concludes our brief introduction to windows. There probably will be a whole slew of books written on Macintosh windows. There are a lot of things we haven't told you and a lot of things we couldn't show you. Hopefully, though, you now understand the basic concept of these windows, and you can at least talk about them at cocktail parties. The window concept is perhaps the most important innovation since the invention of the personal computer. We hope you will take some time to peek in some windows and see if you like what you see.

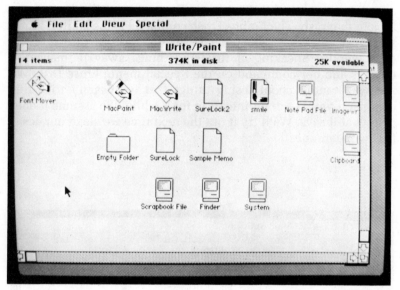

FIGURE 3.31

Chapter 4

Writing, Scribbling and Fixing

The Macintosh may be the greatest word processor of all time — and then, maybe not. We like it. There are some things we don't like about it, though. On the top of the list is the memory problem. It's hard to write the great American novel when the computer is designed for short stories. But, enough of that. This chapter is an introduction to word processing in general. It gives you a good idea of what word processing is, how you can use it in your home and, perhaps more important, in your work. In this chapter, we will tell you what a computer can do, what word processing is and why you might want to do some word processing. We will compare desktop computers to dedicated word processors and tell you what to look for in a word processor.

The Macintosh word processing program, MacWrite, is discussed in the next chapter. If you are already an expert on word processing, you might want to skip this chapter. You're going to miss some good stuff if you do, however.

WHAT IS A COMPUTER

When you think of computers, you may think of them as glorified calculators. Are computers number *crunchers*, machines capable of performing thousands of calculations per second? Sure they are. They have capabilities far beyond the most elaborate desk calculators. At the touch of a key, they can do financial forecasting, loss-and-profit statements, and even inventory lists.

But computers are also for people who use words. This chapter focuses on how you can use computers in creating written material quickly and easily. Using a computer to help you write your own material is called word processing.

WHAT IS WORD PROCESSING?

We probably have you totally confused by now. Three terms are used interchangeably — word processing, word processing program, and word processor. Here is how we will use them:

Word processing. We like to think of this as the function. This is what you are doing. This word is a verb. When you are writing something in this way, you are doing word processing.

Word processing program. This is the program that actually does the work. Any computer used for word processing has a word processing program. This is not as obvious as it may seem. Dedicated word processors have a built-in word processing program. It is instantly available when you turn the machine on.

Word processor. Any computer running a word processing program is a word processor. There is a lot of confusion about this term. Software companies, computer companies, writers, and others sometimes refer to a word processing program as a word processor.

WHAT ARE THE ADVANTAGES OF WORD PROCESSING?

Many people describing word processing tell you how easy it is to enter material. There are some significant advantages. To start with, it is quiet. The only time you make much noise is when you run the printer.

It is also faster. Your effective typing speed will increase dramatically even if you can't type. There are two reasons for this. First, you don't have to worry about errors. Errors are easy to correct, so there is no reason not to type as fast as you can. Second, word processors use something called *word wrap*. The computer automatically wraps any word that won't fit on a line onto the next line. You hit the return key only when you want to end a paragraph. For instance, let's assume you are six characters from the end of the line and you type the word sesquipedalianism. The computer automatically puts sesquipedalianism on the next line. With the typewriter, you might not realize that sesquipedalianism is not going to fit on the line, because the bell doesn't ring until you are five characters from the end. Word processing won't eliminate all the bells and returns in your life, but it helps.

While we agree that *writin'* is important, what's really important is *fixin'*. You can type things with a typewriter at about two thirds the speed that you can type them with a computer, but you may need weeks to correct mistakes. The marvelous thing about a word processor is that you can correct things, move things, delete things and redo things easily and quickly. Have you ever written anything that was really wonderful the first time you read it? But when you went back to read it again, it was awful? Then you started to read through it again and, *voilà*, you found a great introduction on page 7. So you got out the scissors, cut page 7 into three pieces and paper clipped one piece to page 1. And you found other things to cut out and paste. You made a real mess. Then all you had to do was to retype the whole mess.

MacWrite has a command called Cut and another called Paste. You can cut something and paste it wherever you want it. You don't have to do anything with paper. There is no rubber cement, no cellophane tape, no paper clips, no lost pieces and, best of all, no retyping. You can use the cut and paste feature even when you are writing the first draft. Suppose you want to use the word sesquipedalianism in four or five places in your manuscript. You can type sesquipedalianism correctly once and cut it. Then whenever you want to use sesquipedalianism, all you have to do is tell the computer to paste it in. You can use this same technique for sentences, paragraphs or even pages. This could improve your writing, because it lets you easily write difficult things you wouldn't bother to write otherwise. This works great, but we can't think of any possible use for sesquipedalianism.

WHY USE WORD PROCESSING?

If you are not a professional writer and don't aspire to be one, you still may be able to benefit from word processing. You can, of course, write real classy letters to Aunt Gertrude. And you can write term papers, essays, and political speeches. If you are a business executive, or would like to be, you can improve your communication ability. Word processing takes advantage of similarities among business letters and other documents. With word processing, you can produce all those letters identically, or not, as you prefer. But either way, each letter is personalized, as if each one had been independently dictated and typed.

Business Uses of Word Processing

If you are an executive, you may be saying, "Hey, this is great. I'll go out and get my secretary a Macintosh." That's okay, but there may be a couple of things wrong with it. First, you shouldn't talk to yourself while you are reading. Second, you should learn to use the computer yourself. You probably either dictate your letters and memos or scratch them on yellow sheets of lined paper. If you typed them on a word processor, not only would your secretary be able to decipher them but also you would get more work done.

Can a hunt and peck artist learn to operate a word processor? Yes! The computer will wait hours, or days, or weeks for you to hit the next key. You can correct errors by pressing the backspace key or you can have your secretary correct errors. We do both. Back in the old days (1980 or so), we wrote letters and memos the same way you do. We wrote books on a word processor and letters by hand. We weren't sure it was proper for *executives* to type their own letters, but we've been liberated. Now, when we write letters, we save them on disk and put the disk in our *out* baskets. And we get back nicely printed letters with all the errors corrected.

If you start writing your letters on a computer, you may discover there are other things you can do. For instance, you may be able to write memos that don't have to be corrected. Or you may be able to create your own slides, graphs, charts and all kinds of similar things. Whatever you start using the computer for, you will find that it goes faster and easier than it does now.

Multiple copies of documents no longer have to either take all day to duplicate or look like they've been photocopied from a photocopy. With word processing, you can have as many originals as you need within minutes.

Professional Uses of Word Processing

Journalists and authors already know that word processing saves them important time, while improving the quality of their work. Books, magazine articles and newspaper articles all can be written, edited, and printed in any form required.

The adage *time is money* is certainly true for any writer. Word processing saves a phenomenal amount of time and, therefore, a bundle of money. But economics is not the only issue to be considered. You might also discover that the quality of your writing improves with a word processor.

The ability to delete and insert material electronically does much more than speed the writing process. Editing and changing typewritten text is cumbersome. Manuscripts usually end up with masses of red editing marks, and often become useless because it's impossible to follow all the changes and corrections. In addition, it is easy to reject the idea of going through yet another draft and retyping the whole thing, just because it takes too much time.

With word processing, corrections occur as you make them. You don't have to retype anything to see how it looks with revisions. If you want to move a couple of sentences from page 5 to page 10, most word processors let you mark them. Then, with the touch of key, they can be transferred to the new location electronically. Some programs even let you go back to your unrevised version, just in case you decide you like it better.

Your revisions can be accomplished quickly. Therefore, you are likely to do more of them, because the tedious manual tasks have been reduced. You can concentrate on the editing and reworking process rather than worrying about the time it's going to take to retype the material. What takes a couple minutes with word processing would take hours with a typewriter.

Indexes also can be done easily with word processing. You just enter the words and page numbers, then let the program sort everything alphabetically.

DEDICATED VS. DESKTOP COMPUTER

There are basically two kinds of word processors. Some word processors are *dedicated* to word processing. The hardware and software of the system are designed to do word processing only. You can't run data base management or spreadsheet programs on this type of word processor system. The main keyboard looks like a typewriter keyboard, and the keys only produce the letters they stand for. Special function keys are usually found on the top and sides of the main keyboard. These do specific word processing tasks such as add or delete space, move the cursor, move or duplicate portions of material, and save to disk.

A desktop computer has basic hardware that can be adapted to many different kinds of software. You can do not only word processing with it but also a variety of business, home and educational

tasks. The letter keys on the keyboard produce the letters they
stand for. In addition, when they're used with a special control
key, they do other things. Sometimes they even can be programmed
to do a series of tasks.

Does this mean everyone should use a desktop computer as a
word processor? Maybe. Dedicated word processors have one important advantage over desktop computers. They are designed for
a specific function. You *may* get a better screen and you *may* get
more features. We put the emphasis on *may*. Word processing
programs and desktop computers are getting better all the time.

MacWrite and the Macintosh are good examples of how the
technology has improved. The Macintosh could be used as a dedicated word processor. It is as good as most dedicated word processors today, or better. Best of all, it overcomes the two biggest
disadvantages of dedicated word processors — they are inflexible
and expensive. A dedicated word processor can cost you upwards
of $12,000. A similarly equipped Macintosh will cost you about
$4000.

WHAT TO LOOK FOR IN A WORD PROCESSOR

There are many features to look for when you shop for a professional word processor, but these are some of the most important
ones. Remember, a word processor is both a word processing program and a computer. You need to be sure the computer will do
everything the program will and vice versa. For instance, we have
a computer with 512K of memory and a word processing program
that uses 100K of memory. Therefore we should have 412K of
memory available for word processing. It should be that way, but
it isn't. The program is written as if every computer it runs on has
exactly 128K of memory. So we only have 28K of memory available
for word processing. This is a limitation of the program, not the
computer. You won't have this problem with the Macintosh. Mac-
Write uses all the available memory. Which isn't much, by the
way. But we'll talk more about that in the next chapter.

Here are the things to look for:

The more you can see on the screen at once, the better. The
larger the capacity of the screen display, the easier it is to compose
and edit. An excellent word processor has at least a 24-line by
80-character display. In addition, you will probably want to display the effect of special printing codes that underline or print
words in boldface.

A keyboard with many function keys. The more function keys you have, the easier it is to learn and use a word processing program. Most of the special functions can be assigned to a key — just press the key for that operation, and it happens. Without function keys you may have to remember a complicated routine. The Macintosh uses a mouse instead of function keys, so MacWrite is especially easy to use.

Fast, high-capacity, reliable mass storage. Professional word processing calls for reliable, high-capacity disk drives to store documents.

Plenty of RAM. This may or may not be an issue for you. If you type material no longer than a typical business letter, you do not need much memory to hold the document. If you type term papers, reports, magazine articles, or books, however, you'll find it very inconvenient to work on a computer with limited RAM. If you write very long documents, look for a word processing program that uses at least 128K. You can do plenty of work with very little memory, but it's not as convenient, and errors are more likely.

Freedom from glitchitis. *Glitchitis* is a disease found in all sorts of electronic equipment. It generally strikes when a malfunction will do the most damage. It frequently occurs for no known cause and cannot be duplicated when you try to figure out just what happened. Worse yet, it is least likely to happen when you are trying to explain the problem to someone who can fix it.

SUMMARY

You can certainly use a Macintosh for your word processing, but is it the right choice? Perhaps. You may find a larger computer is more suited to your needs.

The Case Against

Most business people and students who could benefit from word processing don't use it — mainly because of the time it takes to learn. Before the Macintosh, learning a word processing program was often a long and frustrating experience. For instance, it is estimated that WordStar, a popular word processing program for IBM PC computers and others, can take three or four months to learn. Few people have been willing and able to invest the 20-40 hours necessary to understand how to use the computer, plus the additional 200 hours or so needed to learn word processing. The

Macintosh has changed that. It takes only a couple of hours to learn how to use the Macintosh, and MacWrite can be learned in about 15 minutes and mastered in a few hours.

A strong competitor to a word processor in a business-secretarial setting is a memory typewriter. Memory typewriters are used in business mostly because they perform better than traditional manual or electric typewriters, and it doesn't take much time to learn to use them. They can hold at least one line of text in memory, and some can save several pages of text in memory for later correction. They are limited, though. You can work with only one line of text at a time, and each line must be accepted or printed before you can go on to the next.

One problem with word processing we need to mention is that it's easy to make *big* mistakes. If something goes wrong, it really *goes wrong*. The most common scenario is sitting down with your word processor and creating a wonderful short story. You near the end of your masterpiece, your heart pounding with excitement and pride. Then, in your frenzy, you accidentally kick the cord of your machine, and unplug it. And because you haven't saved your material, you've lost everything. Unless you've done that at least once, you do not know the true meaning of despair.

Another real time-consuming mistake is when you *search and replace* the wrong thing, automatically replacing one word or number with a different one. Or when you realize too late that you did not mean to replace every single *I* with *we* in a letter. (It makes sense, when you think about it. If you look closely, you'll notice that both of these sentences start with *I*.

The Case For

But don't get us wrong. We think word processors are terrific. Certainly they are a great improvement over the typewriter.

Word processing is easy to use. You don't have to hit the return key every time you come to the end of the line. And you don't have to worry about typing more text than you can get on a single piece of paper (or, for that matter, changing paper). Editing and reediting are easy. You can insert, delete, and move entire blocks of text by touching one key.

Although word processing generally takes time to learn, it pays off quickly. Once you've learned the basics, you can produce better work, in greater amounts, much faster. You'll find the time (and money) you spend is well worth it.

Once you've learned word processing, you're hooked. But that's not bad. You'll continue to find ways word processing can make your life simpler.

Chapter 5

MacWrite

Your reaction to MacWrite is likely to be influenced by your experience with word processing. We were thrilled. But if Mac-Write is the first word processor you've had experience with, expect to be spoiled. You will probably think that, with all word processors, you can: change sentences and paragraphs to various type styles, sizes, and fonts; change margins almost like you do on a typewriter; see format changes as you make them; print exactly what you see on the screen; and do all this with the click of a mouse's button.

LEARNING OVERHEAD

In the last chapter, we mentioned that one of major drawbacks to word processing is the training time or *learning overhead* involved. Some word processors are so difficult to learn that most people just don't bother. If you can type, you can use MacWrite. Basically, all you have to know is how to open MacWrite. You do this by double-clicking the mouse with its tail on the MacWrite icon or by selecting Open from the File menu. When the MacWrite window shown in Figure 5.1 appears on your screen, you begin typing. If you like what you see, you can print it or save it using the File menu shown in Figure 5.2. It should take less than 15 minutes from the time you first see a Macintosh until you can print or save your first document. We don't know of any other word processor you can use this quickly. Once you have learned the basics, there are other things you will want to find out about. We estimate it will take you three or four hours to learn the editing and formatting commands.

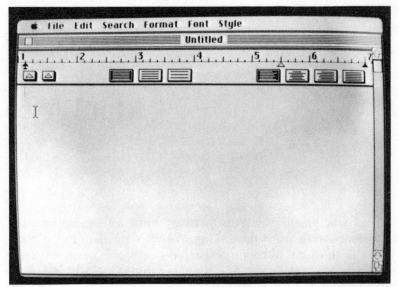

FIGURE 5.1

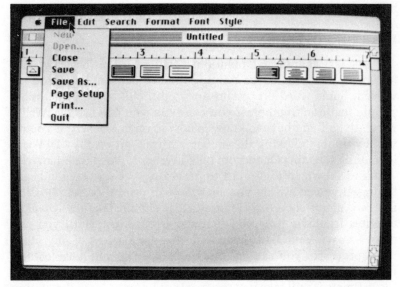

FIGURE 5.2

FORMATS

In computer jargon, *setting the format* of your text means setting your margins, tabs, line spacing, and those kinds of things. At the top of each document, MacWrite displays what looks like an ordinary ruler that controls five formatting functions — margins, indentation, tabs, line spacing, and justification. You can change your text to fit within certain margins by adjusting the position of the two black triangles (markers) on the ruler. Rather than designating margins by commands and complicated formatting tables, as with other word processors, you drag Mac's markers along the ruler with the mouse. When the margin markers are moved, the material below the ruler is instantly readjusted to the new settings. The margins are initially set at one inch and seven inches from the left. In Figure 5.3, we have set them at three inches and six inches so you see them clearly.

The small, arrow-shaped marker at four inches indicates how far the paragraphs are to be indented. You can also reverse-indent, so that the body of the paragraph is indented after the first line. All indentation changes are displayed on the screen as they are made.

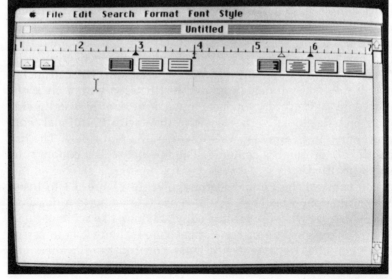

FIGURE 5.3

Tabs are set in much the same way. Each new document comes with a tab marker set at five inches. You drag the marker along the ruler to the place you want to relocate it. You set additional tabs by dragging them out of the tab well, a box on the lower left of the ruler, and placing them where you want them. Even decimal tabs are provided, so you can type numbers with the decimal points aligned.

You have three line-spacing options with MacWrite — single, double, and line-and-a-half. You select one by clicking the appropriate icon in the ruler bar, and you immediately see the new spacing on the screen. The line-spacing icons are on the left starting at the 2½-inch mark.

Four other icons format material as left-justified, right-justified, or left-and-right-justified (full-justified). Left-justified means all words line up on the left side, right-justified means they line up on the right side. Again, you can see your changes as you make them. These icons are on the right side of the ruler.

You can use the formatting features of MacWrite to do interactive experimenting as your material fills the page. So, if you want to write a one-page letter but discover you have two lines too many to fit on the page, you just move the margin markers back until everything fits. You can also reformat your letter to see how it looks double-spaced or centered. If you want to change the format in the middle of your letter, you just insert a second ruler bar and indicate the new settings. Ruler settings also can be copied from one part of your letter to another. You can insert new rulers in the middle of a letter or the middle of a paragraph. You can change margins, spacing, indentation, and justification with a click of a mouse. In other words, you have much more control over the way your material looks with MacWrite than with traditional word processing. In Figure 5.4, we show two different rulers. The text below the top ruler is centered. The text below the bottom ruler is left-justified.

You can use the Format menu shown in Figure 5.5 to insert rulers into your work. You can also use this menu to hide rulers so you can see what the printed copy will look like without them. The primary purpose of the Format menu, though, is to set up how your final document will look. You can have headers and footers. A header is phrase that tells your reader what is on the page. The words and the page number on the top of this page are a header. A footer is the same thing except on the bottom of a page.

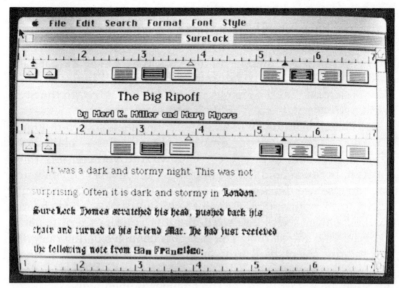

FIGURE 5.4

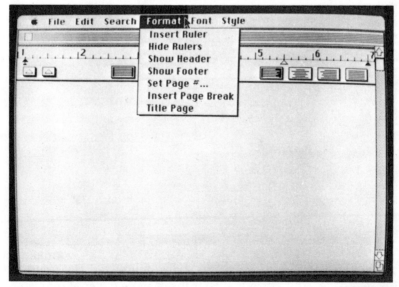

FIGURE 5.5

TYPE SIZES, STYLES AND FONTS

The Macintosh draws all characters on the screen. This means every letter, number and other character can be changed. Therefore, you can use a number of different type styles, formats and sizes. The default, or initial, setting is *12 point, plain text in a New York font*. You can change point size and style with the Style menu and font size with the Font menu.

You can change the style with the Style menu shown in Figure 5.6. You can change among a variety of text styles — plain, bold, italic, underlined, outlined, or shadow. And you can mix these effects to produce bold italic underlined shadow text if you want. You can also use the Style menu to change the type size in a range from 9 to 72 points. (Try 24-point bold italic underlined shadow text!) Whatever styles you set define the appearance of material you type after the setting. You can also change existing material. You simply select part of a document (anything from a single character to the entire body of the text), and make a selection from the Style menu. You can see the changes immediately.

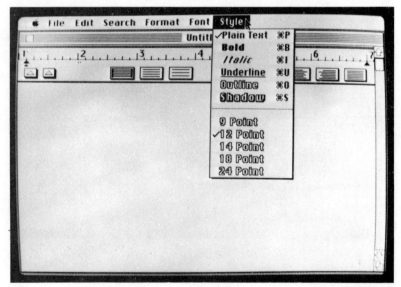

FIGURE 5.6

You can specify different type styles, fonts, and sizes within the same line. And when you later insert more material into your document, the inserted text automatically appears in the style you specified. The Font menu is shown in Figure 5.7.

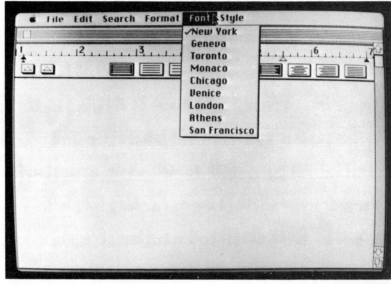

FIGURE 5.7

The best way to describe the Macintosh fonts is to show them to you, so we wrote a mystery story. This is our first attempt at writing mysteries, so we hope you will be patient with us. It will take a lot of patience. The title of the story is in 14-point New York bold. The authors' names are in outlined 9-point Geneva. The text begins with 12-point New York plain and it remains 12-point plain until the next-to-last paragraph. Wherever a city is mentioned, the text immediately changes to the Font that bears the city's name. The next-to-last paragraph is shadowed 12-point New York. The last paragraph is italic underlined 18-point New York bold. Now, for the thrilling adventures of SureLock Homes as told in Figure 5.8.

The Big Ripoff

by Merl K. Miller and Mary Myers

It was a dark and stormy night. This was not

surprising. Often it is dark and stormy in London.

SureLock Homes scratched his head, pushed back his

chair and turned to his friend Mac. He had just recieved the following note from San Fransisco:

A valuable computer manuscript has been stolen from a famous publisher. It is being held for ransom by the Nerds Liberation and Salvation Party. Unless 48 Macintosh computers are delivered to us by wednesday, you will never hear about this manuscript again.

The Athens Society.

"This sounds serious, Mac", said Homes seriously, "perhaps we should go to Geneva."

"But, why Geneva, Homes?" asked Dr. Watt's son.

"Because Geneva is a sans-serif type, Mac," replied Homes, "so there is little or no law there."

"Wouldn't that be sans-sheriff, Homes?" inquired Mac arrestingly.

"Yes, of course, I was just testing you. Actually, we are going to Chicago." replied Homes breezily.

Mac didn't ask about that. Instead, he called Air Canada and booked a flight to Chicago. Naturally, the flight stopped in Toronto.

"My kind of town, Toronto is my kind of town," sang Homes.

"Why is that?" asked the mysterious woman next to him.

"Because, as Mac knows, it has an expanded serif," stated Homes levely.

"Spare me the details," replied the intelligent woman from Monaco.

Homes eyed her carefully. Could she be part of the plot or could she be their client? For the first time in his career, Homes didn't know. But, Homes had other things to think about.

He and Watt's son flew to New York. They checked into the Heartbreak Hotel on 57th Street and began to contemplate the situation. After 28 days, Homes reached a startling conclusion.

"Aha," he exclaimed, "I have now concluded that the culprit is an editor from Venice."

"What makes you think so?" asked Mac startlingly.

"Elementary, my dear Watt's son, the writing on

the envelope is cursive, and only editors from
Venice use cursive writing on envelopes," stated
Homes knowingly.

   "Well, Homes you sure know a lot of things I
don't, but I know something for sure", cried Mac as
he looked out his   New York window.

   **"I'm in the dark about that," said
Homes from the shadows.**

   <u>*We owe Sir Arthur Conan
Doyle an enormous apology,"
said Mac emphatically.*</u>

SPECIAL MACWRITE FEATURES
Editing

   You can edit your work in MacWrite by using the mouse, the
Edit menu shown in Figure 5.9 or both. With conventional word
processing programs, editing and moving items in a document has
required several keystroke commands. Now MacWrite reduces
those commands to a few simple skills using the mouse. Here are
some of the things you can do:

Insert. All material is inserted into your document as you type it.
The insertion point is determined by where you drag it with the
mouse. While inserting, you can't accidentally write over character
you've already typed.

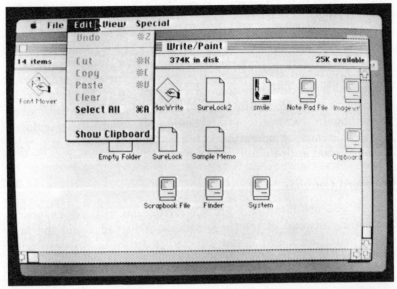

FIGURE 5.9

Backspace. The backspace key moves the insertion point one character to the left while deleting the character to the left. The technical term for this is a destructive backspace key.

Delete. You can delete text in three ways with MacWrite. The backspace key deletes as you move it backwards. You can also delete by selecting part of a document, then choosing Cut from the Edit menu. The cut portion stays in the clipboard for later use. You probably will find the third way the most useful. If you select part of your text and start typing in new text, the selected text will be deleted and the new text inserted simultaneously as you type. If you've badly mangled a word, you don't have to go to great lengths to salvage the correct letters. You only have to select the word by double-clicking the mouse button on it, then retype the whole thing. This tip also applies to short phrases you might want to repair or change.

Undo. This is a marvelous feature. The Undo command in the Edit menu always gives you the option of undoing your last action. You can undo deletes, moves, style changes, and even the last text typed as an insertion. The text of the Undo command changes to reflect your last action. So if you're undoing a Cut command, the prompt will say Undo Cut. If you choose Undo twice in succession, the second time the prompt will say Redo Cut and will undo your previous undo.

Move Text. You can move a block of text in MacWrite by selecting the part of the text you want to move, cutting it to the clipboard via the Edit menu, then pasting the text from the clipboard to your document in its new location. Or you can copy a block of text to the clipboard, and leave the original text in place. Doing this makes the clipboard text available for pasting elsewhere in your document. This moving operation is fairly efficient because it can be accomplished entirely with the mouse.

Keyboard Commands

Once you are familiar with MacWrite, you can use keyboard commands instead of menu selections. You can Undo the last action with *Command Z*, cut selected text to the clipboard with *Command X*, copy with *Command C*, and paste with *Command V*. The Z, X, C, and V keys are on the bottom row of the keyboard, so you can use these four command-key options with one hand. It's a technique Mac writers should quickly develop, because it cuts down on mouse activity and makes text manipulation more efficient.

Search and Replace

The Search menu has commands for finding a specified string of characters and either selectively or universally changing the *find* string to another string. Both functions ignore case. MacWrite's search and replace function is a bit limited. Some other word processing programs allow you to specify whether you want to ignore case or not.

WHAT MACWRITE CAN'T DO

MacWrite is a great word processing program, but there a lot of things it can't do. Here are some limitations. It cannot:

- Store different formats for memos, letters and outlines, then implement them with a single command.
- Edit several documents at once using multiple windows.
- Create footnotes, tables of contents, and indexes automatically.
- Define certain keystrokes to type whole words, phrases or sentences.

- Define a series of program commands into *macro* commands.
- Check your spelling or grammar.

MacWrite's primary limitation is memory. Each MacWrite document is limited to about 27,000 characters, or about 5000 words. That's roughly 20 double-spaced pages. Now that's more than enough space to write your next interoffice memo, but it's barely enough for your short story masterpiece.

The limitation can mostly be attributed to the amount of the Mac's RAM taken up by the programs that control the Mac's desktop and the MacWrite program itself. What's left over in RAM is what you have to work with.

The real limitation, though, is that MacWrite holds your entire document in memory while it's being worked on. Some word processors write portions of a document back to disk when necessary, which means your document's length is limited only by the memory available on your disk.

But for now, you have only a few options. The first is simply to resign yourself to reality and chop up your material into 5000-word sections. This can be annoying, but you can take advantage of MacWrite's other fantastic capabilities right away. The second option you have is to wait until more memory becomes available for the Macintosh. And the third is to wait until another word processing program is developed for the Mac, one that uses the memory storage of a disk. Apple indicates it is working on a more powerful word processing program, so it might be worth the wait. Whatever Apple is working on, it will certainly be similar to MacWrite, so you can't go wrong getting MacWrite now.

Chapter 6

Picasso I Ain't,
But I Got MacPaint

The MacPaint program has so many features that we'd like to tell you about them all at once. Better yet, we'd like to demonstrate them to you in a crash-bang virtuoso performance of MacArtistry. But since that is unfortunately impossible at this moment, we'll just to have to describe it to you. Then you can go to a computer store and experiment with MacPaint yourself. After all, seeing is believing, especially when you are seeing the almost unbelievable!

MacPaint is an entirely new way of thinking of, and creating in, images. It removes some of the barriers surrounding visual design, and gives people who are not trained as artists some of the tools necessary to do a professional job on projects. At the same time, it facilitates design work for professionals. MacPaint eases the basics of design. You don't have to spend time and energy producing dull-but-essential straight lines, circles, shadings, or what-have-you. MacPaint does that instantly for you. And because you can produce these things effortlessly, you gain a tremendous amount of confidence in your final product. This confidence frees the imagination. If you are a non-artist, you dare to try design ideas that would have, before MacPaint, been too ambitious or too tedious. If you are an artist, using MacPaint leaves you with the extra time and resources to explore options, test changes, and refine ideas as never before. What can you do with MacPaint? Communicate in a whole new way. Create smashing graphs and charts. Illustrate memos and papers. Design page layouts. Send unforgettable, worth-a-thousand-words messages. Make your own valentines. See some possibilities? Let's take a closer look.

GETTING STARTED WITH MACPAINT

There are two ways to get started with MacPaint. You can sit down and play with it, or you can go on a guided tour that's included in the program. The tour's okay, but MacPaint is so easy to use you might want to play with the computer some first. If you are looking at the Macintosh in a computer store, you might ask for a demonstration of the guided tour. We'll describe the program's built-in guided tour first. Then we'll lead a little guided tour of our own.

MacPaint's tour begins by showing you how to position and make rectangles that are empty and rectangles that are filled with patterns. It shows you how to choose a pattern and how to use the paint bucket. Next, you are shown how to cut things to the clipboard and how to choose font sizes. The last part of the tour shows you how to use the paintbrush and the spray can. We have two criticisms of the guided tour. It doesn't cover enough, and it is too slow. It is certainly more interesting than television, but you can probably learn more about Macintosh just by playing with it.

MacPaint is used to create pictures, so we will show you a lot of pictures. Let's start with Figure 6.1. It shows the now-familiar desk icons. One of the pictures is a hand with a pen and paper, which is titled MacPaint. This is your entry into the world of MacPaint shown in Figure 6.2.

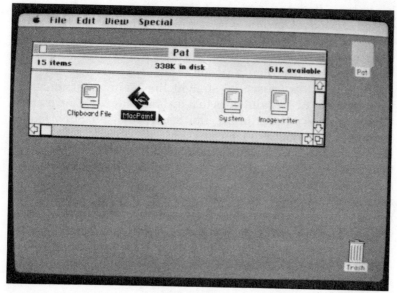

FIGURE 6.1

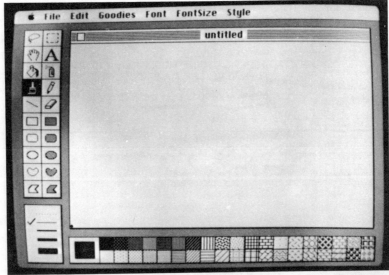

FIGURE 6.2

Now that you are in the MacPaint program, you see the main workspace that takes up most of the screen, the menu on top of the screen, and a bunch of little boxes filled with pictures and patterns on the left and bottom. The pictures on the left are the tool display. And, of course, you see the mouse's tail. The large blank area, where you will create your documents, says *untitled* across the top. Your document won't have a title until you save it and give it a name.

The boxes beside each other on top represent two important ways to move and rearrange things on any document. One is the lasso, and one is the dotted selection box.

The lasso works this way. You click it then move it out to your document. You use it to draw a closed circle around the portion of text or drawing you want moved, as in Figure 6.3. When the circle is closed, the section you have marked begins to pulsate. You can now move it with the mouse's tail as shown in Figure 6.4. If, in addition, you hold down the option key, the encircled part of the document will remain in place but a replica of it can be dragged away within the lasso. The replica will be placed in the document elsewhere when the mouse button and option key are released. You can make as many single copies in this way as you want. (See Figure 6.5.) You also can make multiple copies of anything you are dragging around the screen within the lasso.

FIGURE 6.3

FIGURE 6.4

FIGURE 6.5

Hold down both the option and the command keys while you move the lassoed section around. Replicas of the circled portion of the document will be deposited repeatedly on the screen at intervals determined by how fast you drag the lasso. This creates the remarkable three-dimensional effect shown in Figure 6.6.

The dotted box works in much the same way. Click it, then go to your figure, pull the box around it, then move inside and push the whole box to where you want to reposition it. You can also shrink what you are dragging around by pressing the command key. See Figures 6.7, 6.8 and 6.9. If you click the dotted box twice, it will automatically fit itself around the whole screen.

The main difference between the lasso and the dotted box is that, with the box, you can take as much background with your figure as you want. The amount depends on the size of the box you make. The lasso can move objects of any shape, and moves only the shape, not the background.

When moving and repositioning things on your screen, you'll find the grid command in the Goodies menu (Figure 6.10) to be of help. Choose this command, and anything you move goes along the horizontal and vertical lines of an invisible grid. This can be a big help if you want to reposition an object you moved to its exact former location.

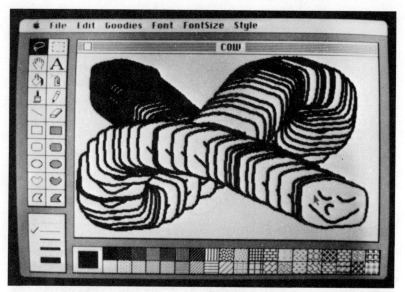

FIGURE 6.6

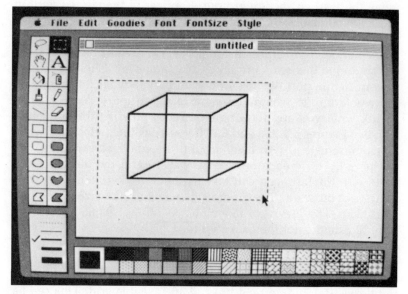

FIGURE 6.7

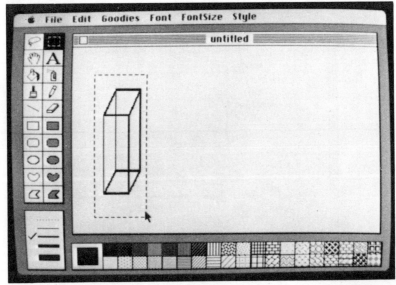

FIGURE 6.8

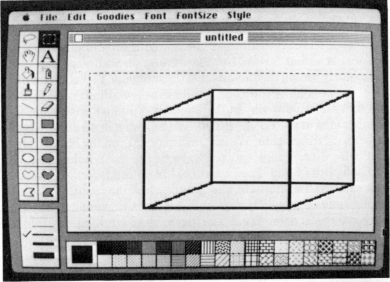

FIGURE 6.9

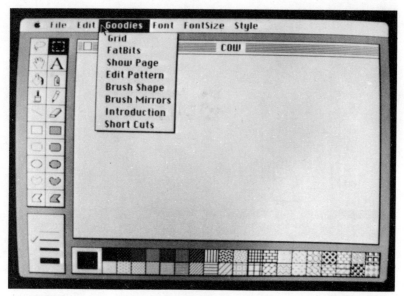

FIGURE 6.10

The third item in the tool display is a little hand. This is used to move and rearrange things on the screen, and also to move the area your screen is viewing. It works like this. The page you are working on, and will print, is roughly eight inches by ten inches. But the Mac's screen normally looks onto only about a third of the area at a time. So you can have things on your page you aren't necessarily seeing on the screen at the moment. You also can push off-screen, with the little hand, things that you don't want to erase but that are in your way at the moment. You just push them into another area of your page, and out of your way, until you are ready to work on them again. We are pushing our drawing off the screen in Figure 6.11. There are two ways to see the whole page. You can select the *Show Page* command from the Goodies menu, or you can use the short-cut and double-click the hand. Either way your whole page will appear as in Figure 6.12, centered horizontally on the screen. What you have been working on, looking squished-up and without very much detail, will be in a dotted box on the displayed page. The dotted box can be moved on the page representation. Whatever is in the dotted box when you click Okay will again fill the screen in detail. With the fill page displayed, you can move the box and anything else on the screen to where you want them. (See Figure 6.13.) This is a tremendous time-saver for designing page layouts. Since it is so easy to rearrange things, you have the time to experiment with layouts that perhaps you wouldn't have tackled before.

The fourth tool you see in the boxes is a big letter A. You click this when you want to put text into your project. A vertical line appears that is the same height as the font size you have chosen. This is where you type your text. The selection of type fonts, sizes and styles works much the same as it does in MacWrite.

The next tool you see is a little paint bucket pouring paint. You use this to put all the patterns you see at the bottom of the page into what you are working on. You pick the pattern you want by moving the mouse's tail to it and clicking. The most recent choice of pattern is always displayed in the big box next to the small pattern boxes. We have put five patterns in boxes in Figure 6.14, and the paint bucket is ready to fill another one. If you don't see exactly what you want, you can modify patterns to suit you by choosing the edit pattern command from the Goodies menu. This lets you gradually change a pattern, or cancel your changes if you haven't really improved things. When you move the paint bucket to the portion you are going to fill in, look carefully to see that there are no tiny gaps or holes in the figure. If there are, the pattern

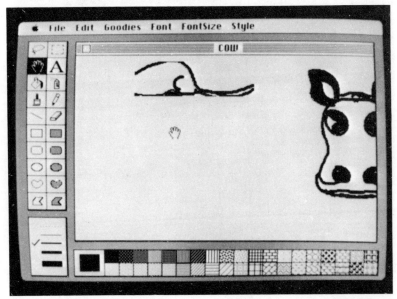

FIGURE 6.11

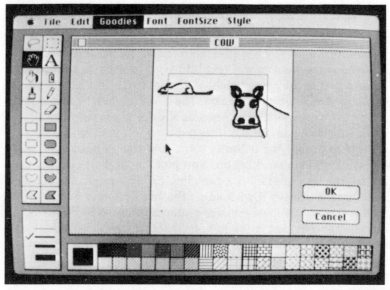

FIGURE 6.12

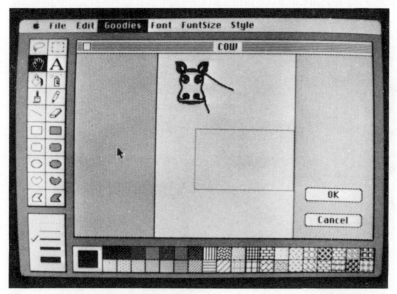

FIGURE 6.13

will escape and color adjacent area. Perhaps you wanted to color one small portion of your project black, and the paint escaped through a tiny gap and turned the whole page black. Disaster! As you can see in Figure 6.15, everything is painted black. Luckily, however, there is a wonderful disaster remedy for those unex-

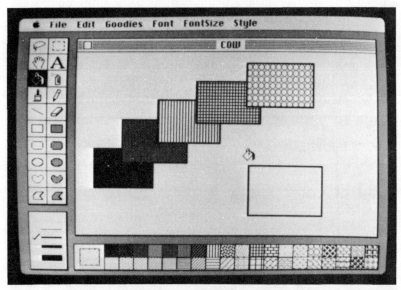

FIGURE 6.14

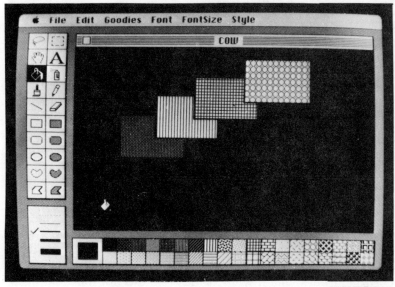

FIGURE 6.15

pected special effects. With the Macintosh you can actually go back in time and retract an action. The Undo command that we've already looked at in the Edit menu is shown in Figure 6.16. This undoes the last thing you did. So if you haven't panicked and pushed keys wildly, you'll be able to make things right again. Click Undo and *presto!* the black paint is back in the bucket.

Next to the paint bucket on the screen of MacPaint is a little can with something that looks like an aerosol spray coming out. In fact, it is a spray can! With this you can spray the screen, and just like with a real spray can, the longer you hold it in one place, the thicker its color goes on. The pattern in the current pattern box is is sprayed on. The spray can makes great bushes and foliage.

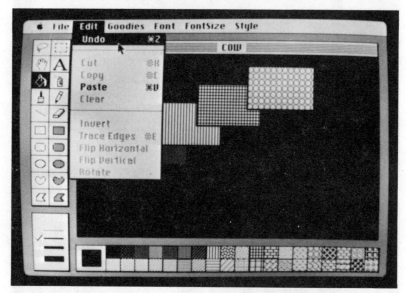

FIGURE 6.16

DRAWING THINGS

Next we look at one of the most versatile tools in MacPaint, and the one you'll spend hours experimenting with — the paintbrush. With the paintbrush, of course, you draw or paint freehand on the screen. The brush draws with any of the patterns. The one that comes out of your brush is the one in the current pattern box.

If you click the paintbrush twice with your mouse, you can choose from the page of brush and nib shapes shown in Figure 6.17. These go from small to big squares, from small to big dots, small to big slanting nibs (both 45 and 90 degrees), vertical and horizontal lines, and a whole series of multi-dot nibs that make

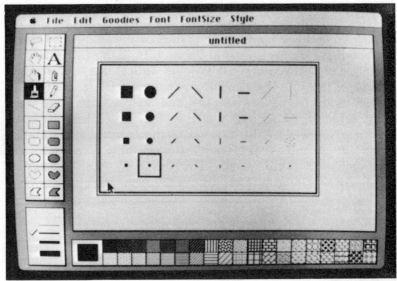

FIGURE 6.17

three to five lines simultaneously. These multi-dot nibs give an amazing three-dimensional look to anything they draw. In Figure 6.18 we have drawn several different lines with the various brush shapes.

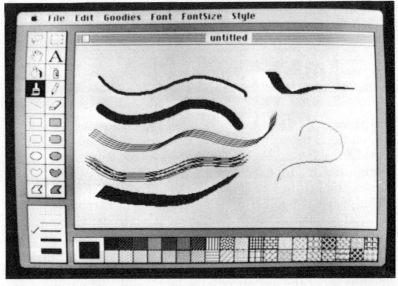

FIGURE 6.18

In addition to the effects you can achieve with these different shapes, you also can use brush mirrors for some truly amazing results. You get brush mirrors from the Goodies menu. The brush mirrors dialog box is shown in Figure 6.19. If, for instance, you point and click the mouse's tail on the vertical line in the center of the box, that line will darken. You have just set up a mirror for the right and left sides of your page. The brush will draw the same thing, reversed, on each side of the page. If you have to draw anything symmetrical, this can make it much easier. When all the mirrors are operating, you have the same thing going on in all eight quadrants of your screen. This gets to be wild! This is one place where we felt confined by the rather small Macintosh screen.

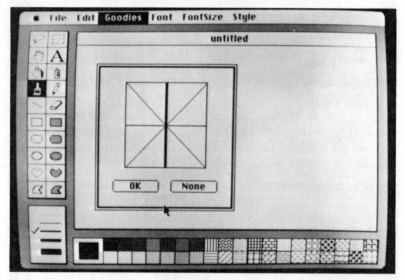

FIGURE 6.19

The patterns we drew got so complex and engrossing we started to want to see them on a big screen. The megalomania of creation started to take over. Figure 6.20 shows a cow being drawn with two mirrors, Figure 6.21 shows a flower being drawn with four mirrors and Figure 6.22 shows all the mirrors at once.

The pencil is another drawing tool at your disposal. At first glance it seems as though the pencil is pretty tame, especially when you have just been exposed to the wonders of the brush. It draws just one kind of line. It also can draw white on any dark background. But where the pencil comes into its own is in fat bits, which is about the neatest refining tool you'll ever come across.

You can select fat bits from the Goodies menu, or you can get them by clicking the pencil twice. Figure 6.23 is a drawing of a French horn. There is a crooked line on the upper right. Figure 6.24 shows fat bits for the flawed section of the drawing. There

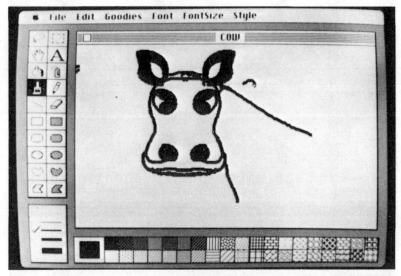

FIGURE 6.20

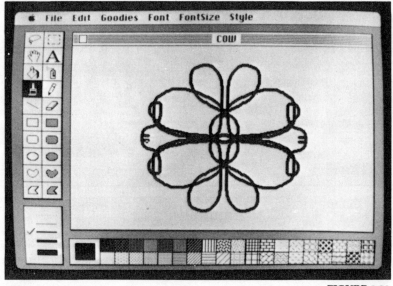

FIGURE 6.21

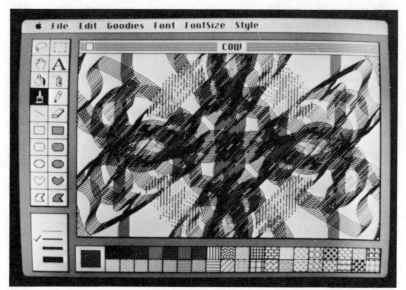

FIGURE 6.22

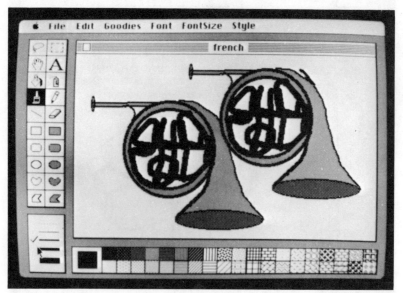

FIGURE 6.23

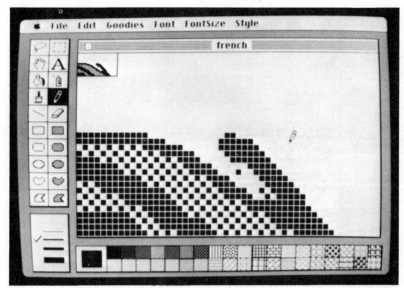

FIGURE 6.24

is a little box in the upper left corner that has a small segment of what is on your screen. On the main body of the screen are a bunch of little black boxes. What *are* these things? Have we turned on some weird kind of pen accidentally? If you look closer, you will see that the shape of the pattern of the boxes seems to correspond to the little segment you see in the corner. If you now take your pen and go over the boxes you'll find you can either erase them or put them back, according to what click you are on. We are removing some of the fat bits in Figure 6.25. If you look to the little corner picture again, you'll see the changes we made have changed part of the picture. What you are doing is fine-tuning your picture, pixel by pixel. If you want to scroll across your whole picture, you hold down the option key and the mouse's tail turns into the little hand in fat bits. You can then move the page to any portion of it you wish to work on.

As you have noticed, we introduced a computer term without defining it. A pixel (or picture element) is a single dot on the screen. When you select fat bits, the Macintosh enlarges the pixels so you can see them. All computers draw things on the screen using pixels. This is not unique to computers. All televisions draw pictures on the screen using pixels. The difference is that a computer uses several hundred pixels, and a television may use several thousand. Still, what you see on the screen is composed of dots.

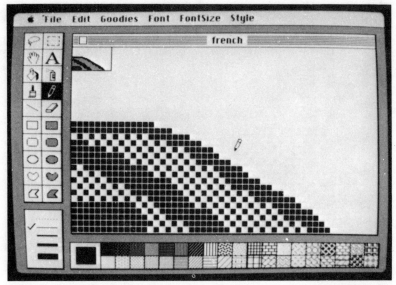

FIGURE 6.25

The Macintosh screen has 512 pixels across and 342 down. Now that you understand what a pixel is, there is one other thing we need to mention. In Chapter 2, we introduced the control panel. We told you the mouse control had two speed settings, 1 and 0. A setting of 0 makes the mouse move across the screen one pixel at a time. A setting of 1 makes the mouse skip every other pixel.

OTHER TOOLS

The diagonal line draws lines, and only lines, from wherever you set it down to wherever you pick it up and put it down again. It acts kind of like the sticky threads a spider uses to build its web. You can also use this tool in conjunction with the shift key to draw *straight* horizontal, vertical and diagonal lines. The shift key acts as a constraint. No matter how crookedly you pull the line across the page, if you are holding down the shift key, the line will end up absolutely straight. With MacPaint, you don't need to worry about being able to draw a straight line. No more rulers!

The eraser is the next tool in the tool kit. Of course, if it is true that what you take out is more important than what you leave in, this is one of the most important tools. Click it once and you can take it out into the screen to erase selectively, or even draw patterns through what you've drawn. Click it twice, and you erase the whole screen. In the heat of creativity, it's relatively easy to run over to the eraser and accidentally click it twice. If this happens, just remember the Undo key in the edit menu, and you're okay.

Automatic Shapes

The next ten boxes have various shapes in them. Half of the shapes are hollow. The other five are the same shapes, but filled with shading. The first two are rectangles. Click either the solid or the hollow rectangle, and you can put it on your page in the size you want. Just keep pulling the mouse along, and the rectangle gets bigger and bigger. You can also flatten, stretch, turn, and otherwise manipulate it with the mouse. But once you click to detach from it, you can't change it again. When you are using any of these shapes, the symbol on the screen that does the drawing is a cross. This helps you position the corner of the figure exactly. It takes a little practice with these to be able to predict which way they are going to grow when you start pulling them. At the bottom of the MacPaint screen is a box with lines of various thicknesses. One of the lines has a check mark by it. This is the menu for selecting how thick you want the lines of the shapes. The heavier the line, the heavier and bigger the cross that does the drawing. You choose the line size by pointing the mouse's tail to the one you want and clicking. If you choose to put the filled rectangle on your page, you will draw it the same way, only it will be filled with the pattern in the current pattern box. Suppose you want a perfect square instead of a rectangle, and you don't want to spend an hour adjusting to get it. Press the shift key (that's the constraining key, remember?) and you will get a square of the size you want. The hexagon and the oval shapes work like the rectangles and have the same features. Press the shift key to get a perfect circle from the oval. Figure 6.26 is a shapes sampler. The shape after the oval is heart-shaped. With this tool you can draw freehand. It is different from the pencil, because you can change the thickness of the line. And, of course, you can draw shapes that fill automatically with a pattern. The last set of shapes are modified trapezoids. You use these in much the same way as the diagonal line works — to draw lines from point to point. Keep in mind that, once you set down the end of the line you are drawing and click the mouse, you can't do anything more to the line (except zap it with the eraser). With a little practice you can draw perfect triangles or other geometric shapes with the trapezoids.

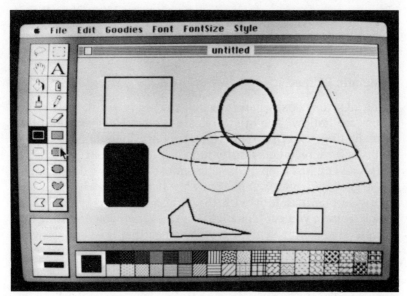

FIGURE 6.26

You might be wondering what you can do with these shapes. Well, for one thing you could become an architect. Maybe someday you could design the new Heartbreak Hotel for your city. The Heartbreak Hotel chain caters primarily to publishers who attend computer conventions. The last one we stayed in is shown in Figure 6.27.

The borders feature is a spinoff of the shapes. You can put a border on anything you have made by drawing a rectangle around it, and then going into the Edit menu and choosing the Trace Edges command. The rectangle, or the shape you are working with, will reproduce its outer edges in a slightly larger size. *Abracadabra,* there is an attractive border suitable for framing where you want it. You can also make a border by putting one color or pattern of shape on the screen, then putting a slightly smaller, differently colored shape inside.

Once you have finished your work in MacPaint, you will want to close. This too is as painless a procedure as you have no doubt begun to expect all Macintosh features to be. Go to the file menu and pick the close command. You will be asked if you wish to save the changes you have made in your file, or if you want to cancel the whole command. If your file is as yet untitled and you say you want to save the changes, you will be asked the name you

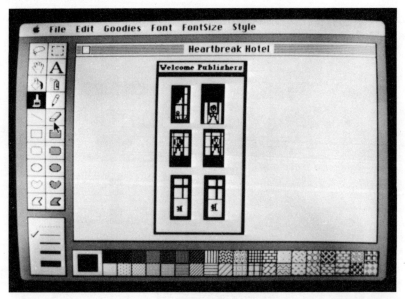

FIGURE 6.27

want to give your document. You type in the name, click save, and you have a new document. After you have your files named and saved, go to file again and move the mouse's tail down to quit. This takes you out to the main desk. Go to file again and down to eject. The disk will pop out, and you can sit back and feel smug. It doesn't matter that you are not Picasso. With MacPaint at your fingertips you can do almost anything.

A SPECIAL THANK YOU

A book like this requires a lot of research and diligence. We couldn't have written this chapter without the help of a special person. We know that you probably didn't read the acknowledgements, but we wanted you to know about Pat Finnegan. Pat drew all the pictures in this chapter except Heartbreak Hotel. She also wrote the rough draft of the chapter. There wasn't any logical place to put her drawing in Figure 6.28, so we decided to put it here. We think it is fitting to end this chapter with Pat's house.

FIGURE 6.28

Chapter 7

MacFuture

There is an old joke in retailing that goes something like this:

    Q: What are the three most important things in retailing?

    A: Location, location, and, of course, location.

A similar comment can be made about computers:

    Q: What are three most important features of a new computer?

    A: Software, software, and, of course, software.

The two most successful computers ever developed, the Apple II and the IBM PC, are successful because a lot of software is available for them. Apple led the way in convincing other companies to write software for Apple computers. Apple surpasses itself with the Macintosh. Every major software company, and many not-as-major software companies, has Macintosh software in the works. In this chapter, we'll discuss what is likely to be available in the next year and why. While hardware enhancements aren't as important as software, they still influence your buying decision, so we will also describe some hardware.

Some of the hardware items we describe in this chapter are already available, but none of the software is. Consequently, we were not able to do in-depth software reviews. Our comments are based on press kit information and interviews with representatives of the companies involved. However, in some cases, we have reviewed the product for other machines and have published these reviews in previous books. For example, we reviewed Multiplan in *Things To Do With Your IBM PC*. We reviewed 1-2-3 in *Computers For Everybody: Third Edition*. We think the Macintosh versions of familiar programs will be easier to use than the versions for other computers that we've reviewed.

SON OF MS-DOS

A computer has something called an operating system. The operating system tells the computer how to print things on the screen, when to run the disk drives, how to run a printer, etc. In other words, the operating system is the program that makes your computer behave differently than an electric clock. You may have noticed that we haven't discussed the Macintosh operating system. Ah, but we did. When we talked about windows, folders and all that stuff in Chapter 4, we were really talking about the operating system. The Apple people have achieved something with the Macintosh that has been talked about for years. The operating system is *transparent to the user*. That means you don't have to know anything about the operating system to use the computer. If you are a computer novice, you should smile pleasantly, nod your head and read on. If you are an experienced computer user, now would be a good time to rub your hands in glee, stand on your desk, and say "YIPPEE!"

You may be wondering what all this has to do with the future. Well, it goes like this. Software developers write programs for popular operating systems. The most popular operating system in the world is something called MS-DOS, developed by Microsoft. It is popular because it is used on the IBM PC and all the IBM PC-compatible computers. For reasons known only to IBM and Microsoft, though, it is called PC-DOS on the IBM PC.

Microsoft had a hand in developing the Macintosh. Apple asked Microsoft for suggestions on how to build the computer. Apple wasn't the first to do this. IBM and Radio Shack also got a little advice from Microsoft. The result of Apple's inquiries is that the Macintosh operating system is somewhat similar to MS-DOS. Although the operating systems are not compatible, there is enough similarity to make program development easier for software developers.

AND THEN THERE'S THE TOOLBOX

As important as the operating system is, it simply doesn't compare to the toolbox. The toolbox, which is part of a software package on the Macintosh ROM, is unique to Apple. You will see some ads that talk about the Macintosh's 64K ROM, or read only memory.

ROM is a good place to put things you want everybody to use. The contents of ROM can't be changed, so games, programming languages and things like that often come on ROM. If you own a video game, you already have some ROM. Video game cartridges are ROM. You can't store anything on them. All you can do is put them in your video game player and play the game. The video game player is a computer. It reads the contents of the ROM into its internal memory and displays the results on your TV screen. The Macintosh does that and a lot more.

Three programs are in Mac's ROM — the operating system, Quickdraw, and the User Interface Toolbox. Quickdraw draws all screen graphics and can be accessed by programmers. The toolbox is almost another operating system. It is a window that opens into the workings of the computer. This means a programmer can save a lot of time in writing programs for the Macintosh. In addition, all Macintosh programs can use the desk accessories, the clipboard and the editing functions. These combinations will make programming faster and easier. Consequently, there will be plenty of software available for the Macintosh. Another factor also will affect how much software becomes available for the Macintosh. The Macintosh is based on *Lisa* technology, so it is relatively easy for programmers to convert existing Lisa programs to the Macintosh. Apple has sold about 20,000 Lisa computers, and there are three new models. We'll take a quick look at the Lisa computers before we describe the Macintosh hardware and software.

APPLE 32 SUPERMICROS

The Macintosh is one of a series of Apple computers called the 32 Supermicros. The three other computers in the series are Lisa 2, Lisa 2/5, and Lisa 2/10. The new Lisa computers all use a 3½-inch disk drive, identical to the drive in the Macintosh. All three Lisas also have 512K of memory. The Lisa 2/5 also has a five-megabyte hard disk. This is an important feature. You can store about 400,000 characters on a 3½-inch diskette. You can store about five million characters on a five-megabyte hard disk. The Lisa 2/10 has a ten-megabyte hard disk. The Lisa computers range from about $3,500 up to about twice as expensive as the Macintosh, but they have a lot more memory and storage. In addition, some good software already is available for the Lisa machines.

PRODUCTIVITY SOFTWARE

The Macintosh is first and foremost a business computer. The target audience is mid-level managers and people who aspire to be mid-level managers. A manager is primarily concerned with controlling information. Software used to control information is usually called productivity software. Common examples are spreadsheet programs, word processing programs and project management programs. We have already reviewed two productivity programs, MacWrite and MacPaint, so let's start here with similar programs.

Microsoft Word. This word processing program is somewhat similar to MacWrite. It uses scroll boxes to view material, command keys as short cuts and the edit menu for things like cut and paste. However, you can do some things with Word that you can't do with MacWrite. For instance, you can search for a page number, and you can automatically create a glossary. It is available from Microsoft for $200.

MacDraw. MacDraw is a structured graphics program published by Apple. You can use it to prepare organization charts, flow charts, graphs and technical drawings. The major difference between this program and MacPaint is you can work with four documents at a time with MacDraw. It sells for $125.

Memowriter. This is a word processing program designed for memo writing. You can mix words and numbers and still total the numbers. For example, you can use it to prepare the following invoice;

Beans	2 pounds	.69	$	1.38
Computer				1956.23
Gingham	6 yards	5.89		35.34
Computers For Everybody				9.95
		Total		2002.90

Memowriter is published by dilithium Press and should be available in the third quarter of 1984. Tentative price is $49.95.

Spreadsheets

Accountants, financial vice presidents, bank loan officers and other finance professionals have used spreadsheets for a long time. The electronic spreadsheet is a computer version of the accountant's workpad. People use spreadsheets because they are an easy, convenient way to keep track of numbers. Early spreadsheet programs, such as VisiCalc, had some of the same limitations as the manual workpads — but there were significant differences. The primary difference is that you can change things on an electronic spreadsheet without erasing, as you must on a manual workpad. If you've ever written a column of numbers, run a total, then changed an entry, you know how frustrating that can be. If you enter your column into an electronic spreadsheet, the total changes automatically when you change an entry. Now, imagine several hundred columns. You can manipulate data in several thousand different places at one time! This means you can do *what if* analyses quickly and conveniently. If anything you do involves numbers, then you should look carefully at spreadsheets. The amount of time they can save you is almost unbelievable.

Multiplan. Multiplan was the first spreadsheet program announced for the Macintosh. We have reviewed Multiplan for other books, and we have never been all that impressed with it. However, the Macintosh version is quite a bit better than other versions. Multiplan, like all other spreadsheets, divides the spreadsheet into rows and columns. Each junction of a row and column is called a cell. It is easy to picture this if you draw a series of vertical lines on lined paper. Your vertical lines combine with the horizontal lines already there to form boxes. You can do the same thing with a conventional electronic spreadsheet, except that you have to imagine the lines. Multiplan on the Macintosh, however, actually draws the lines. In addition, Multiplan takes advantage of unique Macintosh features such as the Finder and the mouse. Multiplan is published by Microsoft, so it operates quickly and efficiently. It sells for $195.

1-2-3. When we wrote this book, Lotus 1-2-3 was still in development for the Macintosh. It is the most popular spreadsheet program available for personal computers. We can't describe something we haven't seen, but we can tell you that 1-2-3 is an excellent program

on other machines. It's strongest feature is the thought that went
into how people actually use computers. This is also the strongest
feature of the Macintosh, so 1-2-3 on the Macintosh should be a
fantastic program.

Other Productivity Software

TeloFacts. TeloFacts is the version for the Macintosh of dilithium
Press' TeloFacts. Figure 7.1 shows a TeloFacts menu. This program
will help you evaluate questionnaires. It is used by marketing
organizations to conduct polls and by bankers to evaluate loan
applications. It can evaluate anything involving multiple choice
questions. You can use it to rank, score or list individual respon-

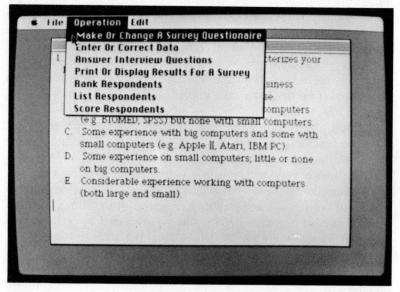

FIGURE 7.1

dents. For instance, assume you are a personnel manager assigned
to hire a new cost accounting manager. You have 150 applications.
The first question on your questionnaire checks an applicant's
experience. You can tell TeloFacts to assign a different weight to
each answer. If an applicant has cost accounting experience, you
might say that is worth six points. If the applicant has no accounting experience, you might say that is worth no points. You can
do this same thing with each question. Then you can interview
the ten candidates with the highest scores. TeloFacts will be available in the third quarter of 1984 and will sell for $100.

PFS:FILE. This is a data base program or, in other words, an electronic file manager. You can record, store, update, retrieve and sort information. Every line of information in your file is a field you can manipulate. A person's name, street address, city, state, postal Zip code, and country all can be different fields. So, if you want to find everyone you sold beans to on Aquatic Drive in French's Forest, Sydney, Australia, you easily get a list. You can use it to do things like sort listed products by price or date of first production. Or you can use it to keep track of all the times you sang at the Met. For the Macintosh, it will be available from Software Publishing Corporation in the second quarter of 1984. It will sell for $100.

Think Tank. You might call this the ultimate creative program for the ultimate creative computer. Think Tank is an outline processing program. (See Figure 7.2.) Have you ever jotted an outline or a bunch of notes for an idea you had, then revised the notes? Think Tank will help you organize your ideas into a coherent pattern. It won't do your thinking for you, but it will free you to be more creative. It will be available in the third quarter of 1984 from Living Videotext.

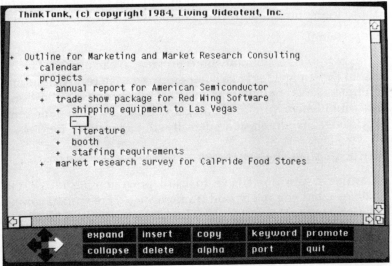

FIGURE 7.2

COMMUNICATIONS SOFTWARE

CommQuest

CommQuest is a group of program modules available from di-lithium Press. You can use the programs individually or combine them. They should be available in the fall of 1984.

You can use **Chat** to access information utilities such as The Source and CompuServe. (If you are unfamiliar with information utilities, you might want to read "The Outer Limits: Communicating with the World." This is Chapter 5 of *Computers For Everybody: Third Edition.*) Chat will sell for $29.95.

Send Receive is a data communication module. You can use it to communicate with other computers. For instance, if you have a document created on an IBM PC that you want to use on your Macintosh, you can use this program to transfer the information both ways. It will sell for $39.95.

You can use **Message Minder** to watch your electronic mail box. It will send and receive messages unattended. It will sell for $49.95.

Cipher is an add-on module. It will help you encrypt and decrypt information before and after transmission. You can use it to start your own bank, go into competition with the CIA or send secret memos to the president of your company. It will sell for $19.95.

MacTerminal

This is Apple's communications program. It can turn the Macintosh into a terminal for large computers. You can receive information from a large computer then paste it into various applications. This could be very useful if you get information from your company's large mainframe computer. It will be available for $99.

PROGRAMMING LANGUAGES

Obviously, you don't have to learn programming to use the Macintosh, but you might find it interesting. Three programming languages are available for the Macintosh — Logo, BASIC and Pascal.

Logo is a children's language developed at Massachusetts Institute of Technology. If you have ever seen five-year-olds play with Logo on a computer, you know the true meaning of humility. Logo is graphics-oriented and extremely easy to use. Logo graphics are drawn by moving a turtle symbol on the screen. On the Macintosh, you use the mouse to move the turtle. Kids will love this concept, and you may find it interesting also. By giving commands to the turtle, you can draw a square. By grouping commands, you can make what programmers call a statement. When you can write simple statements, you can write simple programs. Most children can learn to write simple programs in ten or fifteen minutes. Macintosh Logo will be available from Apple in early summer of 1984 for $99.

BASIC is the most popular programming language ever developed. Its popularity lies in its ease of use. Most commands in BASIC resemble what you want to do. For example, PRINT means print something on the computer's screen or printer. Two versions of BASIC are available for the Macintosh. Apple sells MacBASIC, and Microsoft sells MBASIC.

Every two or three years, programmers discover a new wonder language. The process is somewhat akin to pharmaceutical companies discovering new wonder drugs. The new language, so its developers say, is going to be the be-all and the end-all, and everyone is going to learn to program. Pascal is a wonder language. It is a much more sophisticated language than BASIC or Logo and, consequently, is more difficult to learn. However, if you want to learn the inner workings of the Macintosh, you will need to learn Pascal. If you are a programmer, you will be pleased to know that Apple's MacPascal takes full advantage of the programmer's toolbox. The toolbox gives you access to the Finder, which means you can easily write Macintosh programs that use Finder menus, icons and so on.

MAGAZINES AND BOOKS

At least 20 books are being written about the Macintosh. All the major computer book publishers have at least one in the works. Our publisher, dilithium Press, has two besides this one. *How to Use the Apple Macintosh* by Jerry Willis will get started with Mac applications. *The Macintosh Apple* by Kenneth C. Green and Rika Van Dam is a comprehensive user's guide for the Macintosh. It will give an in-depth look at the desktop manager, MacWrite, MacPaint and other programs. We are coauthoring another book with Jerry Willis that will expand the material covered in this chapter. *Things to do with Your Macintosh Computer* will be published in the fall of 1984 by Signet.

David Bunnell is one of the most knowledgeable computer magazine publishers. He was in on the development of the first microcomputer, the Mits Altair 8800. His new magazine *MacWorld* looks like a real winner. He has pulled together a good group of experienced magazine and book authors to put out a slick publication that sells for $4. We were quite impressed with the first issue.

HARDWARE

Apple is producing several hardware add-ons for the Macintosh. Other companies also are working on such products. Rather than try to describe each product individually, we'll give you an overview starting with the Apple products. We might be stretching it a bit to call the soft-sided carrying case a hardware product, but we didn't know where else to include it. If you are going to carry your Macintosh around, you will want this $99 case. If you plan to do financial analysis or anything else that involves a lot of numeric entry, Apple sells a six-inch by four-inch numeric keypad for $99. Apple also sells 3½-inch diskettes, a security kit and a modem. The modem will connect your Macintosh to another computer over phone lines. It sells for $225.

Although you can effectively use the Macintosh with one disk drive, you will find your productivity increases if you have two. Apple sells the second disk drive for $495. Davong Systems plans to introduce 5-, 10-, 21-, and 32-megabyte hard disk systems in 1984. The five million characters stored by a five-megabyte hard disk system is equivalent to about 40 books the size of this one. The complete works of Louis L'Amour and all revisions and all his bank accounts would fit on a 32-megabyte computer. Tecmar has developed a five-megabyte hard disk system as part of its Candy Apple product line. Tecmar also is working on a modem and some other equipment with which you can connect your Macintosh to other computers.

If the Macintosh is as popular as the Apple II, and we think it will be, there will more hardware and software products than we could list in ten books this size. (In fact, the software and hardware directories for the Apple II equal about ten books this size.) You should be able to do anything you want with a Macintosh.

This concludes *Presenting the Macintosh*. We hope you have found it interesting and informative. More importantly, though, we hope it has piqued your interest in the Macintosh. We think it is a great computer! If you buy a Macintosh, please share your experiences with us. You can write us in care of dilithium Press. Happy computing.

Glossary

The computer business is infested with jargon. There is a bug in many computer companies. They simply don't put it into their RAM that you don't understand jargon. But, enough of that. The purpose of this glossary is to introduce you to some computer terms you may encounter when you shop for computers. Not everything in this glossary relates to the Macintosh. When you shop for a computer you'll need some basis for comparison, so we have included some jargon commonly used with other computers. Before you give up in despair, keep in mind that terms like brake pedal, speedometer, gearshift, and radio are also jargon. They just represent another way of getting there.

Active window   The top window on the Macintosh desktop. Files can be moved from the active window or manipulated while they are in the active window.

Alphanumeric   Combined alphabetic and numeric form, for example, a mailing list. The numbers 0-9 and the letters A-Z or any combination.

Applications program   A program designed to perform a specific task. Applications programs can be games, educational programs, or business programs. For instance, MacWrite, MacFacts and MacPaint all are applications programs.

Arithmetic expression   A group of letters, numbers, symbols or any combination of those that tells a computer to perform an arithmetic function. For example:

$$2+2$$
$$2*2$$
$$A22$$

2/4
2/A
A*(2/B8)

Arithmetic operator   A symbol that tells a computer to perform addition (+), subtraction (−), multiplication (*), division or raise to a power (∧).

ASCII   American Standard Code for Information Interchange. Numbers that represent to computers the letters, numbers and other symbols that are communicated through them. For example, when you type a on the keyboard of your computer, the binary number 01 100001 is sent to the computer's central processing unit (CPU). The CPU then displays the letter a on the screen.

Assembly language   A low-level programming language that is much faster than a high-level language such as BASIC. Assembly language programs are extremely difficult to write. Here are two lines from an assembly language program:

    LDA
    MOV C,A

Back up   To make an extra copy of a file or disk. A backup copy is intended primarily to keep people from going insane over the loss or anticipated loss of material they've stored.

BASIC   Beginner's All-purpose Symbolic Instruction Code. A high-level computer language designed for beginners. Here are four lines of a program written in BASIC.

    10 PRINT "HELLO HOW ARE YOU?"
    20 DIM A$ (10)
    30 INPUT A$
    40 GOSUB 500

Baud   A unit used to express the speed of information transfer. In microcomputers, a baud is one bit per second.

Baud rate   The rate at which information is transferred. For instance, 300 baud is a transfer rate of 300 bits per second. Each character, space, or symbol requires eight bits. Therefore, a baud rate of 300 transfers 37.5 characters per second. At that rate, if you are sending a letter with each word approximately six characters long and you have one space between words, you can send about five words a second or 300 words a minute.

Binary number   A number system that uses only two digits, 0 and 1, to express all numeric values. See digital computer.

Bit   The basic unit of computer memory. It is short for binary digit and can have a value of either 1 or 0.

Black box   A piece of equipment that is viewed only in terms of its input and output.

Break   To interrupt execution of a program.

Buffer   A temporary storage place used to hold data within a computer for further processing.

Bug   A problem that causes a computer or computer program to perform incorrectly or not at all.

Byte   A group of eight bits usually treated as a unit. It takes one byte to store a unit of information. For instance the word love requires four bytes.

CAI   Computer-aided instruction.

Canned software   One or more programs ready to run "as is."

Cathode ray tube (CRT)   The picture tube of a television set or monitor. It is used to display computer output.

Central processing unit (CPU)   The heart of a computer. It contains the circuits that control the execution of instructions.

Click   The process of pressing the mouse button.

Close   To indicate to the computer that you are through working with a file, document or window.

Code   A system of symbols and rules for representing, transmitting, and storing information.

Coding   Writing a computer program.

Command   An instruction that tells the computer to perform an operation immediately. Macintosh commands usually are part of a menu. However, they can be evoked with a combination of the command key and a letter key.

Command key   A special Macintosh key that combines with other keys to tell the computer what to do.

Computer-aided instruction (CAI)   Teaching done with the use of a computer. Such a system of individualized instruction uses a computer program as the teaching medium.

Control key   A special key always used in conjunction with another key. It can be used to tell a computer to stop operation or to perform a special function. The Macintosh command key is a control key.

CPU   Central processing unit.

CRT   Cathode ray tube.

Cursor   A little, flashing rectangle that indicates where the next character will be displayed on a CRT being used for computer text display.

Cut   To remove text or graphics from a document.

Daisy wheel printer   A printing machine with a print head that has a number of radial arms or petals, usually 96. Each petal has a type character on the end. Daisy wheel type is equal to or better than most typewriter type.

Data   All items of information a computer can process or generate — numbers, letters, symbols, facts, statements, etc.

Data base   The entire collection of data in a computer system that can be accessed at one time.

Data base management system   A program that organizes data in computer storage so that several, or all, programs can have access to virtually any item, and yet a particular item need be keyed into the computer system only once.

Data processing   Converting data into a form that a machine can read so a computer can work on it.

Data transmission rate   Baud rate.

Debug   To eliminate errors in a computer or computer program.

Decimal number system   The commonly used number system based on ten digits, that is 0-9.

Default   See default value.

Default value   An assigned quantity for a device or program that is set by the manufacturer. A default value in a program is usually the most common or safest answer.

Desk accessories   An unique Macintosh application program that gives you seven commonly used desk aids, for example, a calculator.

Desktop   A corollary for the Macintosh electronic work environment.

Desktop computer   A complete computer system designed to fit on a desktop. The Macintosh is a desktop computer.

Device   Any piece of computer equipment.

Digital   A system that uses the numbers 0 and 1 to represent variables involved in calculation. This means that information can be represented by a series of offs (0s) or ons (1s). See bit.

Digital computer   A computer that uses a series of electronic offs and ons to represent information. These offs and ons are converted to or from binary numbers. The Macintosh is a digital computer.

Disc   Disk

Disk   A piece of flat, circular plastic coated with magnetic material that is rotated when used to store computer information. See also hard disk and diskette.

Disk drive   An electromechanical device that stores information on a disk or recalls information from a disk.

Diskette   A small, portable computer disk. Diskette sizes are determined by diameter. The most common sizes are 3½ inches, 5¼ inches and 8 inches. The Macintosh uses 3½-inch diskettes.

Disk operating system (DOS)   An operating system that lets a computer use one or more disk drives. See operating system.

Document   A computer file, i.e., a letter, a picture, a SureLock Homes mystery.

Documentation   All available information about a particular computer, computer program, or set of programs. It would include instructions on how to turn on the computer, how to load programs, and so on. For a computer program, documentation should include what computers the program runs on, how much memory is needed, and how to operate the program.

DOS   Disk operating system.

Dot matrix printer   A printer that forms characters as pattern of dots. The dots lie within a grid of definite dimensions, such as five dots by seven dots.

Double-click   The process of pushing the Macintosh mouse button twice to issue a command.

Edit   To make changes on the screen in data or a program.

Electronic mail   Personal or other messages generated on one computer and transmitted to another computer at a different location. The computers are connected by phone lines.

External memory   Mass storage.

Field   A unit of information that is part of a file. For instance, in the following mailing list file, NAME, ADDRESS, CITY, STATE, and ZIP are all fields:

       NAME_____

       ADDRESS_____

       CITY_____

       STATE_____

       ZIP_____

In the example above, the title and the information following it constitute a field. For instance, the field for Joe Jones is: NAME Joe Jones.

File   An organized collection of data. As used in this book, a file can be a document, a program or any other collection of data stored on diskette or used in a computer.

Finder   A special Macintosh applications program that helps organize other Macintosh applications programs. Its primary purpose is to arrange the desktop.

Font   A typeface, for example, one of those that can selected by a Macintosh applications program.

FORTRAN   Formula Translation. A high-level computer language used for mathematical or engineering applications. Here are three lines from a FORTRAN program:

```
40 FORMAT (E14.7)
X = A + B*C/D-E
WRITE (6, 50)X
```

Graphics   Pictures, line drawings, and special characters that can be displayed on a screen or produced by a printer.

Hard copy   A copy of the computer's output printed on paper.

Hard disk   A mass storage device that uses a rotating rigid disk made of a hard plastic-like material. It has many times the storage capacity of a diskette.

Hardware   Physical components of a computer system, such as the computer itself, the printer, keyboard, and monitor.

High-level language   A computer language that uses simple English words to represent computer commands. For instance, the command PRINT "Hello" in BASIC tells the computer to print the word *Hello* on the screen.

Icon   As used with the Macintosh, this is a pictorial representation of an object, concept, file, or message.

Initialize   To set a program element or hardware device to an initial quantity, usually zero.

Input   To transfer data from the keyboard or a mass storage device into the computer's internal memory.

Input device   A device used to enter information into a computer. These are all input devices: keyboard, joystick, disk drive, cassette player.

Input-Output   The process of entering data into a computer or taking it out.

Integrated circuit   A group of components that form a complete miniaturized electronic circuit. The circuit has a number of transistors plus associated circuits. These components are fabricated together on a single piece of semiconductor material.

Interactive   A computer system that responds immediately to user input.

Interface   A device that allows other devices to communicate with each other — a modem, for instance.

Inverse video   A process that shows dark text on a light background on a display screen. Normally, light text is shown on a dark background.

I/O   Input-Output

Jack   A plug socket on a computer.

K   When used as a measure of computer memory K is an abbreviation for kilobyte or kilobytes. It is also an abbreviation for kilo.

Kilo   A prefix meaning 1000. In computer jargon it is used as an abbreviation for 1024.

Kilobyte   1024 bytes. Thus 4 kilobytes (abbreviated 4K) of memory is about 4000 bytes of memory. It is exactly 4096 bytes, but 4K is a convenient way to keep track of it. This means that 4K of memory is enough space for 4096 characters, spaces, numbers, and symbols in a computer.

Language   The means of communicating. The difference between computer language and human language is that a computer language allows humans to communicate with computers. The lowest level of language is machine language, the pure language of the computer. Machine language programs use 1s and 0s to represent the ons and offs in the computer. Machine language programs are the most difficult to write but they do not have the speed and action limitations of higher level languages. Assembly language programs also are low-level languages, but they use simple mnemonic statements as commands. High-level languages — such as BASIC, FORTRAN, and Logo — use English-like statements to tell the computer what to do. BASIC is the most common language because it is the simplest to use.

Load   The process of entering data or programs from an external device, such as a disk drive, into the computer. Once you *load* a program into a computer, it is available for use.

Logo   A high-level computer language that is often used by children. An easy-to-learn language, Logo allows colorful, detailed graphics to be drawn on the screen. Sprite graphics and turtle graphics are terms associated with Logo.

Low-level language   A computer language at the machine level (a pattern of pure binary coding). It is neither simple nor obvious for a human being to read, understand, or use.

Machine language   The lowest-level language. It is a pattern of ones and zeros that the computer understands.

Mainframe computer   A large, expensive computer generally used for data processing in large corporations and government installations. Originally, the phrase referred to the extensive array of large rack and panel cabinets that held thousands of vacuum tubes in early computers.

Mass storage   Files of computer data stored on media other than computer memory. For example, diskettes and cassettes are mass storage devices.

Matrix printer   Dot matrix printer.

Mega   A prefix meaning one million.

Memory   The internal hardware in the computer that stores information for further use.

Menu   A display shown on the screen that gives a list of options. On the Macintosh, an option is selected either by highlighting it and pressing the mouse button or by pressing the command key in conjunction with a letter key.

Microcomputer   A fully operational computer that uses a microprocessor as its CPU. Microcomputers are a new kind of computer. Whereas minicomputers are small-scale versions of large computers, microcomputers are an outgrowth of semiconductor technology. Consequently, some microcomputers have features not found on either minicomputers or mainframe computers.

Microprocessor   A central processing unit contained on a single silicon chip.

Minicomputer   A small computer based on large computer technology.

Modem   A modulating and demodulating device. It links computers together over telephone lines.

Monitor   A television or cathode ray tube used to display computer information. In common usage, a monitor usually refers to a special device used exclusively for computer output. It can display a line 80 characters long and has at least 24 lines of text.

Mouse   A small hand-held computer input device. It has a metal ball on the underside. When the mouse is slid so the ball rotates, signals are sent to the computer. These signals are changed to like movement of parts of the screen display. The Macintosh mouse is shown in Figure G.1.

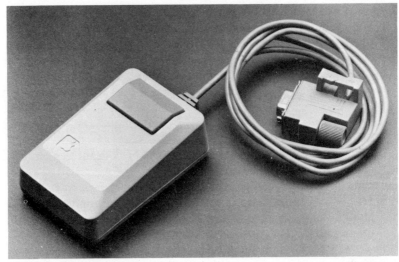

Mouse button A push button on the top or side of a computer mouse that indicates data entry. See also click and double-click.

Mouse's tail As used in this book, the arrow that appears on the Macintosh screen that indicates where the next action will take place. It is controlled by movement of the mouse.

Nano One billionth.

Nanosecond One billionth of a second. Modern computers operate in nanoseconds.

Network A means of connecting computers together so that information can be shared.

Numeric data Data that consists entirely of numbers.

Open To make a computer file or window available for use.

Operating system A set of computer programs devoted to the operation of the computer itself. The operating system must be present in the computer before applications programs can be loaded or run.

Option key A special Macintosh control key.

OS Operating system.

Output Information or data transferred from the internal memory of the computer to some external device.

Output device A device used to take information out of a computer. CRTs, mass storage devices (such as disk drives), and printers are all output devices.

Pascal   A powerful high-level computer language for business and general use. Named for French mathematician and philosopher Blaise Pascal (1623-1662). Here are three lines from a Pascal program:

```
BEGIN
READLN(I,HOURS)
IF I = 1 THEN WORK: = SUN
```

PC   Personal computer.

Peripheral   Any device that connects to a computer. Printers, joysticks, and modems are peripherals.

Personal computer   Microcomputer.

PILOT   This is an easy-to-learn, high-level language designed for novice computer users. It is used primarily for educational programs.

Pixel   A picture element that is one point on a screen. The size of the pixel depends on the computer graphics mode being used and the resolution capabilities of the screen.

Printer   A device for producing paper copies (hard copy) of the data output by a computer.

Program   An organized group of instructions that tells a computer what to do. A program must be in a language a computer understands.

Prompt   A symbol, usually a question mark, that appears on a screen to ask that information be entered.

QWERTY   An abbreviation used to indicate a standard typewriter-style keyboard. The first six letters in the second row of a standard keyboard are QWERTY.

RAM   Random access memory.

Random access memory (RAM)   The read-write memory available for use in the computer. Through random access, the computer can retrieve or send information instantly at any memory address. See memory.

Read   To take data from a storage device, such as a diskette, and put it into a computer's memory.

Read only memory (ROM)   Random access memory that contains permanently stored information. The contents of this memory are set during manufacture. A game cartridge is read only memory.

Read-Write memory   Computer memory into which data can be put or from which data can be taken at any time.

Resolution   Clarity of picture as represented by the number of points (or pixels) that can be put on a television screen (or monitor) both vertically and horizontally. High-resolution indicates a large number of pixels and, therefore, a sharper display.

Reverse video   Inverse video.

ROM   Read only memory.

Save   A command that tells the computer to store the contents of memory on some medium, such as a diskette or cassette.

Screen   A CRT or television screen.

Serial   A group of events that happen one at a time in sequence. For instance, a serial interface reads in a byte one bit at a time. Modems transmit data serially.

Silicon   A nonmetallic chemical element resembling carbon. It is used in the manufacture of transistors, solar cells, etc.

Software   The programs and data used to control a computer. Software is available in many forms. A software program can be typed in or transmitted over a telephone. It also may be available on cassette, diskette, or cartridge.

System   All the hardware components that make a computer usable, such as the computer, printer, modem, keyboard, CRT, and disk drive or cassette player.

Turtle   A small, triangular shape displayed on a screen in the use of turtle graphics with Logo language. The turtle shows the direction of lines for graphics. For example, if an instruction says move north, the turtle moves toward the top of the screen.

Users' manual   A book or notebook that describes how to use a piece of computer equipment or software.

Video display   The screen of a monitor or TV.

Window   A special box on a computer screen that shows what is available in either the computer's memory or from diskette.

Word processing   A special feature of a computer that provides for manipulation of text. See also word processor or text editor.

Word processor   A computer program that provides for manipulation of text. It can be used for writing documents, inserting or changing words, paragraphs or pages, and printing documents.

Write   To store data on external media such as a disk or cassette. The expression *write to diskette* means that the information stored in the computer's memory is sent to the diskette, where it is stored.

Write protect   A method of fixing a disk so that no additional information can be stored on it. When new material is written to a diskette, old material there may be erased.

Index

MORE HELPFUL WORDS
FOR YOU from dilithium Press

Bits, Bytes and Buzzwords
Mark Garetz

This book translates all the computer jargon you've been hearing into words you can understand. It explains microcomputers, software and peripherals in a way that makes sense, so your buying decisions are easier and smarter.

ISBN 0-88056-111-4   *160 pages*   *$7.95*

COMPUTERS FOR EVERYBODY™, 3RD EDITION
Jerry Willis and Merl Miller

In a clear, understandable way, this new edition explains how a computer can be used in your home, office or at school. If you're anxious to buy a computer, use one, or just want to find out about them, read this book first!

ISBN 0-88056-131-9   *368 pages*   *$9.95*

COMPUTERS FOR EVERYBODY™ 1984 BUYER'S GUIDE
Jerry Willis and Merl Miller

Here's a single source for up-to-date information on microcomputers. This book tells you everything you need to know about computer and software buying, including in-depth comparisons of 143 computer models.

ISBN 0-88056-132-7   *592 pages*   *paper $19.95*

Instant (Freeze-Dried Computer Programming in) BASIC—2nd Astounding! Edition
Jerald R. Brown

Here is an active, easy, painless way to learn BASIC. This primer and workbook gives you a fast, working familiarity with the real basics of BASIC. It is one of the smoothest and best-tested instructional sequences going!

ISBN 0-918398-57-6   *200 pages*   *$12.95*

BRAINFOOD — Our catalog listing of over 130 microcomputer books covering software, hardware, business applications, general computer literacy and programming languages.

dilithium Press books are available at your local bookstore or computer store. If there is not a bookstore or computer store in your area, charge your order on VISA or MC by calling our toll-free number, (800) 547-1842.

Send to: dilithium Press, P.O. Box E, Beaverton, OR 97075

Please send me the book(s) I have checked. I understand that if I'm not fully satisfied I can return the book(s) within 10 days for full and prompt refund.

___ Bits, Bytes, and Buzzwords $7.95

___ Computers For Everybody, 3rd Edition $9.95

___ Computers For Everybody 1984 Buyer's Guide $19.95

___ Instant (Freeze-Dried Computer Programming in) BASIC — 2nd Astounding! Edition $12.95

☐ Check enclosed $ _____
Payable to dilithium Press

☐ Please charge my
VISA ☐   MASTERCHARGE ☐

_____ Exp. Date _____

Name _____

Address _____

City, State, Zip _____

Signature _____

☐ Send me your catalog, Brainfood.